Practical AI for Healthcare Professionals

Machine Learning with Numpy, Scikit-learn, and TensorFlow

Abhinav Suri

Apress®

Practical AI for Healthcare Professionals: Machine Learning with Numpy, Scikit-learn, and TensorFlow

Abhinav Suri
San Antonio, TX, USA

ISBN-13 (pbk): 978-1-4842-7779-9   ISBN-13 (electronic): 978-1-4842-7780-5
https://doi.org/10.1007/978-1-4842-7780-5

Managing Director, Apress Media LLC: Welmoed Spahr
Acquisitions Editor: Aaron Black
Development Editor: James Markham
Coordinating Editor: Jessica Vakili

Distributed to the book trade worldwide by Springer Science+Business Media New York, 233 Spring Street, 6th Floor, New York, NY 10013. Phone 1-800-SPRINGER, fax (201) 348-4505, e-mail orders-ny@springer-sbm.com, or visit www.springeronline.com. Apress Media, LLC is a California LLC and the sole member (owner) is Springer Science + Business Media Finance Inc (SSBM Finance Inc). SSBM Finance Inc is a **Delaware** corporation.

For information on translations, please e-mail booktranslations@springernature.com; for reprint, paperback, or audio rights, please e-mail bookpermissions@springernature.com.

Apress titles may be purchased in bulk for academic, corporate, or promotional use. eBook versions and licenses are also available for most titles. For more information, reference our Print and eBook Bulk Sales web page at http://www.apress.com/bulk-sales.

Any source code or other supplementary material referenced by the author in this book is available to readers on GitHub via the book's product page, located at www.apress.com/978-1-4842-7779-9. For more detailed information, please visit http://www.apress.com/source-code.

Printed on acid-free paper

This book is dedicated to all the mentors and friends who have given me support throughout my education and beyond. A special thank you goes to my parents, whom I cannot thank enough for encouraging me and helping me down this path. Sic Itur Ad Astra.

Table of Contents

About the Author

Abhinav Suri is a current medical student at the UCLA David Geffen School of Medicine. He completed his undergraduate degree at the University of Pennsylvania with majors in Computer Science and Biology. He also completed a master's degree in Public Health (MPH in Epidemiology) at Columbia University Mailman School of Public Health. Abhi has been dedicated to exploring the intersection between computer science and medicine. As an undergraduate, he carried out and directed research on deep learning algorithms for the automated detection of vertebral deformities and the detection of genetic factors that increase risk of COPD. His public health research focused on opioid usage trends in NY State and the development/utilization of geospatial dashboards for monitoring demographic disease trends in the COVID-19 pandemic.

Outside of classes and research, Abhi is an avid programmer and has made applications that address healthcare worker access in Tanzania, aid the discovery process for anti-wage theft cases, and facilitate access to arts classes in underfunded school districts. He also developed (and currently maintains) a popular open source repository, Flask Base, which has over 2,000 stars on GitHub. He also enjoys teaching (lectured a course on JavaScript) and writing. So far, his authored articles and videos have reached over 200,000 people across a variety of platforms.

About the Technical Reviewer

Vishwesh Ravi Shrimali graduated in 2018 from BITS Pilani, where he studied mechanical engineering. Since then, he has worked with BigVision LLC on deep learning and computer vision and was involved in creating official OpenCV AI courses. Currently, he is working at Mercedes Benz Research and Development India Pvt. Ltd. He has a keen interest in programming and AI and has applied that interest in mechanical engineering projects. He has also written multiple blogs on OpenCV and deep learning on LearnOpenCV, a leading blog on computer vision. He has also coauthored *Machine Learning for OpenCV 4* (Second Edition) by Packt. When he is not writing blogs or working on projects, he likes to go on long walks or play his acoustic guitar.

Foreword to *Practical AI for Healthcare Professionals*

Over the years ahead, artificial intelligence (AI) will play an ever-increasing and ultimately a transformative role for medicine's future. Nearly every week, we are seeing peer-reviewed studies that demonstrate the potential of deep neural networks for improving the accuracy of interpretation of medical images, from scans to slides to skin abnormalities to real-time machine vision pickup of colon polyps during endoscopy. Beyond medical images, algorithms are getting validated for patients, capturing their own data, coupled with algorithmic assistance, to facilitate the diagnosis of heart rhythm abnormalities, urinary tract infections, ear infections in children, and many other common reasons that would require a visit to a doctor. This early phase of medical AI will inevitably progress with validation via prospective and randomized clinical trials that are sorely lacking at this juncture. As Antonio de Leva wrote in *The Lancet*, "Machines will not replace physicians, but physicians using AI will soon replace those not using it."

But how will physicians get up to speed and learn about this field, which has undergone so much rapid change in the past decade owing to the subtype of AI known as deep learning (DL)? In this new book, Abhinav Suri, a medical student at UCLA, has provided an outstanding primer for uninitiated clinicians. Abhinav has the perfect background for this: a double degree in computer science and biology from Penn, an MPH degree from Columbia, and additional experience leading medical scan AI research at the Perelman School of Medicine. In just seven chapters, he succinctly lays out the basics and delineates the limits and potential flaws of AI, the different types of machine learning (ML) algorithms and deep neural networks, and "snake oil" AI. We've needed such a book for the medical community to get grounded, not so that physicians can code, but rather to understand the power, nuances, and limitations as AI makes its way deeper into the practice of medicine.

Undoubtedly, we will see more educational tools to help promote understanding and optimal use of AI in healthcare over the years ahead. The main textbook of the overall field is *Deep Learning* by Ian Goodfellow and colleagues, but it is quite comprehensive and well suited for people who intend to code and get deep into neural networks. Suri's new book sets a very good standard for the goal of getting a quick and pragmatic introduction into AI, catering to the specific needs of clinicians. It will get you to "think like a computer" which is a requisite step to get grounded. Awareness of the basics and nuances of AI will eventually become a standard part of every medical school curriculum, and this primer may be considered a very good start in that direction.

—Eric J. Topol, MD
Professor and EVP of Scripps Research
Author, Deep Medicine
La Jolla, California

## CHAPTER 1

Introduction to AI and Its Use Cases

In the healthcare world, talk about artificial intelligence (AI) has been increasing over the past few years. As a result, healthcare professionals are strongly considering the usage of this remarkable tool in creating novel solutions that could benefit clinicians and patients alike. Yet, in the process of developing these applications, individuals are often confronted with several questions, perhaps the most important of which is "Do I really need AI?" To answer that question, one has to understand what AI is beyond the high-level. Unfortunately, the vast majority of beginner-facing resources on AI stop at the generalized overview of AI and do not talk about how to implement it. The more advanced materials suffer from being opaque, are mathematically dense, and often are addressed to an audience of seasoned programmers and computer scientists. The purpose of this book is to give you, the reader, an understanding of what AI actually is, how it works, and how to code AI-based algorithms in a manner that is approachable to a beginner (with a background in healthcare/medicine). But before we can get into the details of AI and its mechanisms, we need to establish a ground-truth definition of what AI actually is and establish the logic behind what kinds of problems would benefit from an AI approach. With that in mind, let's get started by talking about a paradox that the world of healthcare is facing: too much information and no idea what to do with it.

© Abhinav Suri 2022
A. Suri, *Practical AI for Healthcare Professionals*,
https://doi.org/10.1007/978-1-4842-7780-5_1

The Healthcare Information Paradox

The world of healthcare is becoming increasingly technical. Working with the likes of electronic health record, patient management, and picture and imaging archival systems means that the previous pen-and-paper method of keeping patient notes has gone the way of the dodo. However, these new methods of tracking patient data means that healthcare institutions now have a way to process all of this digitized information in a less burdensome manner. Just two decades ago, the idea of even doing a study analyzing large swaths of patient data at a single institution was daunting since individual patient reports would have to be transcribed, collated, grouped together (if there were multiple visits), standardized in some manner, filtered for irrelevant conditions, and more. Now, if a researcher or healthcare worker wants to gather information on a set of patients, the beginning steps for that analysis are just a few clicks away.

That is great news, but what do we do with that information? If we have data on every facet of a given patient's medical history, how does a researcher even determine what factors are relevant to analyze? For example, if someone wants to predict whether a patient is likely to develop diabetes or not, the first few factors to turn to would be their blood glucose content, age, and weight. But are those all the factors? Can we gather more information regarding their family history? How about their BMI instead of just their weight? What about HbA1c? What about information regarding their prior conditions, diet, frequency of ER visits, proximity to grocery stores, and more? All of these factors could contribute to the likelihood of someone developing diabetes. However, when we try to come up with a set of "Yes/No" statements to figure out if someone is likely to develop a certain condition, it quickly becomes infeasible for a person to determine which of these factors significantly contribute and how one factor interacts with another.

This is the point where technologies in the field of artificial intelligence (AI) may come in handy. Specifically, these algorithms can "learn" how to make decisions about risk status, weighting each of the characteristics we have on patients to maximize the overall accuracy of predictions. This approach illustrates how AI can help solve medically related problems (here, the problem of predicting risk). But AI may not necessarily be the best solution in all cases. We really need to understand what AI is and when it would be most appropriate to actually use it before we can even think about using coding to tackle medical problems that may necessitate the usage of AI.

AI, ML, Deep Learning, Big Data: What Do the Buzzwords Mean?

So we've talked about the term "AI" a little bit so far, but an immediate question that comes to mind is, "What is AI?" That question is a little bit difficult to answer without going into how non-AI programs work.

Imagine you have to calculate a patient's BMI. By definition, this is just weight(kg)/(height(m))^2. It is a very simple calculation that anyone can do by hand. If given weight in pounds and inches, we can apply the CDC recommended formula of 703 * weight(lbs)/(height(in))^2. Since we know the exact formula to calculate this quantity, reporting a patient's BMI is as simple as inputting the patient's weight and height into a calculator and reporting the number. This is something we could easily do without AI because it is a simple calculation with already set parameters. If we need to determine if someone is underweight, normal, overweight, or obese, we report their status according to the CDC guidelines (underweight if BMI < 18.5, normal if BMI is ≥ 18.5 and < 25, overweight if ≥ 25 and < 30, obese if ≥ 30). For simplicity sake, let's write out what we've covered so far:

```
Given Weight_in_kg, height_in_m:
    BMI = Weight_in_kg / ((height_in_m)^2)
    if BMI < 18.5:
        then Patient is underweight
          otherwise if 18.5 ≤ BMI < 25:
        then Patient is normal
            otherwise if 25 ≤ BMI < 30:
        then Patient is overweight
    otherwise if BMI > 30:
        then Patient is obese
```

Believe it or not, this is our first "program" (in quotes because you can't actually run this on a computer, yet). Regardless, this algorithm (a.k.a. a set of steps) has a number of features that can distinguish it from AI. First, none of the parameters about what defines certain boundaries of a patient's weight status change. Those are explicitly set per CDC guidelines. Additionally, we know that no matter how many times we carry out this algorithm, the result will not change.

A program made with technologies in the field of AI typically does not come with parameters that are hard-set. Rather, an AI program will attempt to "learn" necessary parameters to optimize achieving some end goal. When I say "learn," I really do mean learn. Typical approaches to AI involve giving an AI program a set of training data, "telling" the program to optimize some metric, and then evaluating the performance of the program on testing data that was not used to train it (basically giving it a test just as a student would take in school). Framed in the context of our BMI problem from before, an AI approach to this problem would involve giving an AI program a list of hundreds (potentially thousands) of patients with their weight, height, and ultimate BMI status (underweight, normal, overweight, obese). Through the process of training, the AI program will attempt to learn relevant parameters to output the correct weight category. We can then evaluate the accuracy of the program on a set of testing data that was not used to train the program. Why do we do this testing step? To make sure that the program actually learned to generalize its calculations beyond the training data it had seen. The differences between normal programs and AI programs are highlighted in Figure 1-1.

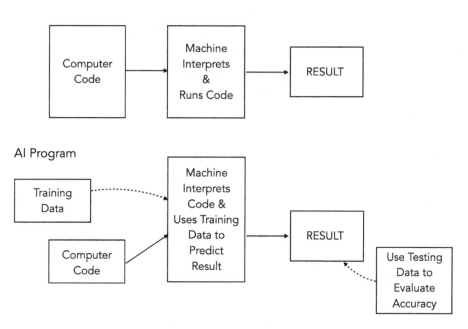

Figure 1-1. *Shows the primary difference between a normal program and an AI program. Note the involvement of training and testing data in the AI program*

The details of how the AI program executes the earlier example will be elucidated later on in this book, but some salient concepts can be gathered from the previous scenario. First, in an AI program, the program itself attempts to improve its performance according to some metric we specify. Second, in an AI program, since we do not specify parameters, we should use some form of training and testing data to ensure that the program learns how to optimize the main metric and has generalized beyond data it has already seen during the learning process. If we peek into what the AI program learns, we do not necessarily have a guarantee that it has formed a similar decision-making process to ours. All we do know is that it performs at some accuracy relative to our metric.

Let's think of a less contrived example for where AI might be used. How would one go about detecting, from a brain scan, whether a patient has a tumor? For a radiologist, this is an easy task. Pull up an MRI from a PACS system and look for abnormalities in the scan. Okay, now how would I detect if 1000 patients have tumors in their scans? Well, off-loading that work onto one radiologist or even a team of radiologists would still mean that this task takes a while to do. To speed it up, we might consider the idea of using a program to do this. But how do we specify to the program how to look for a tumor? We can't necessarily give it experience from several years of medical school and residency training. We also can't take the non-AI approach from earlier because each individual patient probably doesn't have a brain tumor in the exact same location in an MRI series nor will all the tumors look the same (on top of the fact that MRIs could have been taken with different imaging parameters, etc.). So our only real solution left is to do this task with AI.

There are some AI algorithms out there (called neural networks) that can learn how to detect objects in a scan and even do more complex tasks such as segmentation (i.e., marking exactly which pixels/voxels in an image correspond to a certain object, in our case, a brain tumor). However, the process will be the same. We will train the AI program with some annotated data MRI scans (i.e., scans that show exactly what parts of an MRI slice contain a tumor if one exists), test it on some data the algorithm hasn't seen before to evaluate its accuracy, and then run that trained AI program (often interchangeably referred to as a "model") on our 1000 images. Again, we do not know exactly how the AI does this process and what exactly it will look for (though we can do some tricks to visualize some parts of the program), but we do know that it does its job at a certain level of accuracy (as determined by its performance on the testing data and our 1000 scans).

Now that we have a basic understanding of what is and isn't AI, let's clarify a formal-ish definition for artificial intelligence. Roughly AI is just intelligence that is demonstrated by machines. It encompasses most of the processes out there that involve some pattern of a learning/training phase and then testing/evaluation of the resulting program. We will ultimately see that what is currently referred to as AI is not real intelligence as you and I would think about it. Rather, in most cases that are applicable for medical imaging and studies, AI can be thought of as advanced pattern recognition. In the examples earlier, our AI programs were tasked with recognizing patterns in BMI and weight categorization and finding patterns in MRIs that would be indicative of tumors being present. However, current forms of AI that exist can carry out more complicated tasks such as processing human speech, creating human-like conversations, playing human games, and so on. To date, advancements in this field have focused on performing specific tasks very well; however, it has not made many strides in developing a machine intelligence that is generalizable beyond a specific task (however who knows what could happen in the future).

Alright, so that is AI. Now what is machine learning? Machine learning can be defined as a set of algorithms that gets better with experience. When I say "experience," I mean that the results of the program itself will change and optimize according to some final metric (in most cases, this is some form of accuracy) when exposed to enough training data. Machine learning is a subset of artificial intelligence. Common machine learning algorithms out there include linear regression (yes, that type of linear regression that you use in excel to make a line of best fit for some data). In the case of linear regression, we do not necessarily have a distinction between training and testing data; however, we are trying to get a best guess at the actual line of best fit for whatever data is given to us. Through a specific algorithm, a program can iteratively refine that guess over multiple iterations before it reports back a result that is "good enough" (which may or may not be the optimal line of best fit for the data). Other machine learning algorithms out there include decision trees (which will effectively make flow charts for determining what category a given input belongs to given some attributes about that input), clustering algorithms (which try to group points into a prespecified number of groups), and instance-based algorithms (which attempt to predict labels based on the unknown point's proximity to prior training data).

Deep learning, another term you may have heard of, accomplishes the same task as machine learning; however, it uses a specific set of algorithms that involve the use of artificial neurons which operate in a similar way to our own neurons. Just as a single neuron in our body has a behavior of an action potential, so to do these artificial neurons. These artificial neurons are interconnected since the output of one feeds into the input of another, leading to the accumulation of signals across multiple groups of neurons (called layers). The more layers a network has, the "deeper" it becomes and the more capable it is to learn more salient information from the training data that allows it to generalize beyond the training dataset. There's also another subset of deep learning called natural language processing (NLP) that can aid in the processing, interpretation, and generation of text data by computers. Deep learning algorithms are ones that encompass a large portion of the major advances in AI today (or at least the advances that are talked about most often). Because of the versatility of neural networks and the vast amount of computational power available to us now (compared to two decades ago), deep learning algorithms have become incredibly useful to industry and research, aiding in tasks such as object detection from images, text generation for human-like conversations, and more. These algorithms are shown in Figure 1-2.

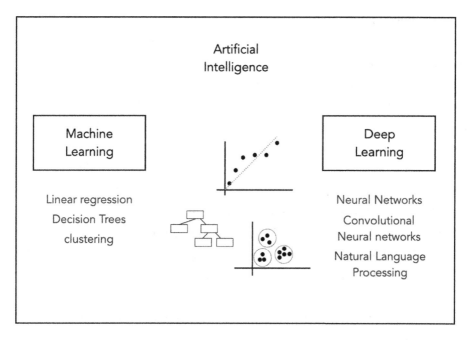

Figure 1-2. *Overview of AI and examples of algorithms in the fields of machine learning and deep learning*

Common to deep learning and machine learning is how problems are structured. Learning algorithms can be classified as supervised or unsupervised (there are some additional categories, but they are not relevant for this book).

Supervised algorithms are ones that require humans to provide labels of the training data itself. In our BMI example, we had to provide a weight class label for a given individual to train the network and to evaluate its accuracy. Supervised algorithms typically involve any classification tasks (e.g., asking the program to determine what weight class an individual belongs) or a regression task (e.g., asking what is the line of best fit for some set of data).

Unsupervised algorithms are ones that do not require any individual labeling for data points. Instead, we ask for the program itself to come up with a grouping for individual data points in our training data.

For example, if I were to reframe the BMI problem to instead ask the program to classify everyone into four general groups without giving any real input as to what those groups may be, that would be an unsupervised learning task. Another type of unsupervised learning task is known as dimensionality reduction which effectively is asking a program to determine what are the x most important features in a given data that would allow us to explain all of the variance in the data.

However, all of these tasks require data to actually get the algorithm to perform well (recall that machine learning algorithms iteratively improve based on the training data available to it). However, for some of these algorithms (particularly neural networks), the amount of data required for a trained model to perform well can be large (some might even say "big"), which brings us to the next question: what is "big data"?

It is hard to pin down an exact definition of "big data" itself or even figure a single unifying definition for the term. However, one thing that is clear is that it is being used more commonly these days. As the wealth of information on the Internet increases and as individual organizations gather more and more data points about their users and visitors, it behooves researchers, programmers, and analysts to begin to figure out what insights can be gathered from millions of data points of individuals. Effectively, "big data" and its associated science, "data science," revolve around trying to look for a signal in the noise by performing operations on large datasets to extract useful insights. Data science operations do not necessarily need to employ AI methods in their analysis at all and instead can extract meaningful results from statistical measures such as mean, median, range, percentiles, and more. However, data science and AI methodologies play well together since data science is focused on extracting information from seemingly incomprehensible data and subsets of AI are focused on doing the same thing, but with some fancier iterative learning methods. Combined together, these two worlds yield advanced pattern recognition programs that perform well in a variety of scenarios.

So now you know what AI, machine learning (ML), deep learning (DL), and big data/data science actually mean. We will now move onto seeing how approaching a problem from an AI perspective actually looks like and what considerations we need to take into account as we plan the training, evaluation, and deployment of the eventual program we develop.

AI Considerations

Well, one thing you'll need is a conception of the exact question you are trying to answer. And, ironically, that involves asking more questions. The first of which is to ask yourself how you normally (i.e., without the aid of an AI) solve this problem. From there, determine how much that procedure changes based on different case parameters and see whether that solution still holds. If you are able to find a general approach that works, it might be worth reducing your AI problem to trying to emulate that process. For example, in the case of finding a vertebral fracture, it is necessary to measure three vertebral heights for each vertebral body. The relative differences between these heights are enough to classify fracture type and severity. So, it stands to reason that our AI should probably also attempt to do the same thing, that is, find all of the vertebral bodies in an imaging study and measure the three vertebral heights necessary for fracture detection. In this case, the data we would use to train the AI would be the locations of vertebral bodies and heights for each of the vertebral bodies. But just providing those inputs alone (i.e., coordinates corresponding to a bounding box location of a vertebral body and a list of three height measurements) can still produce uncertainty around where those heights should come from. However, if we train the neural network to find six key points associated with forming the three lines that measure height, we can just calculate the distance between the key points. In general, changing a problem from something that is nebulous to more concrete and limited in scope can help you determine a better approach to AI problems.

After you form a general sense around what a specific problem should be, your next step is to try and find data that can help the neural network train. There is no one correct answer to the amount of data you would need; however, it is helpful to look at previous attempts to solve the problem you are attempting, but in other domains. For example, the spine fracture problem I mentioned in the last paragraph could be solved by looking at a group of AI models focused on determining where humans are in photos and where the head, hands, feet, hips, torso, and knees were for each human. It turns out that class of research projects was able to take advantage of a concept known as "transfer learning" (effectively using a trained part of another AI model) to drastically cut down on the number of training samples needed from thousands to hundreds. These data can also be augmented (i.e., copied and manipulated in some way) to artificially produce more training data that mimics other conditions that may be underrepresented in the training dataset available to you (e.g., in the case of MR images, you might want to augment training data with images of different brightness and contrast values to account for changes in imaging parameters).

After you have secured a dataset, your next task would be to quantify the performance of the network. I will discuss the implications of "AI snake oil" in the last chapter of this book, but be forewarned it is incredibly easy to pass off a really high accuracy rate as an accomplishment when that accuracy rate lacks external validity due to selection biases present in your training and testing dataset or how you constructed the network. Furthermore, if you are in the position where you are considering using an existing AI solution, you should be forewarned that some vendors tend to take on the usage of the term "AI" as a buzzword instead of truly using machine learning or neural networks to produce their outputs.

Training and deploying your network will also require computational power and a fair amount of it depending on the task you are dealing with. Some AI can be trained using your laptop alone. Others will require that you somehow have access to higher-powered computational resources. Thankfully, there are solutions out there that are free for most experimental purposes (and cost money to host upon deployment or need for greater resources). Once your AI is trained, you will also need to take care of how it will be deployed (i.e., how will the ultimate user of the AI be able to interact with it). In the medical setting, deployment is a huge concern because there will be a number of systems you may need to interact with in order to create a streamlined experience for your end user. Additionally, as a tool that could potentially be used on the management of patients and healthcare data, you need to explore the role of FDA regulations and statutes around your potential AI-based solution (and should consult with appropriate professionals on that front).

Lastly, and most importantly, concerns about the privacy of patient data and biases in the dataset should be addressed before starting to train or distribute your AI solutions. In some instances, it is possible to glean information about the underlying dataset used to train an AI model from outputs the model itself. For example, if you were to be creating an AI-driven chatbot that was trained on texts/emails with healthcare staff, it is possible that a neural network could accidentally output sensitive patient information since there is a nonzero possibility that an AI could "see" that information as valuable in performing its ultimate task. Additionally, along the lines of biases in your dataset, it should be noted that outputs from the AI reflect the data that was used to train it. If you were to create an application that detects melanomas on the skin and your dataset is comprised primarily of light-skinned individuals, there is a non-negligible chance that your network outputs could be biased to output more accurate results for light-skinned people and different results for darker-skinned people. Accordingly, care should be taken to balance the dataset used as much as possible across multiple categories, which will also help with achieving high external validity.

Summary

So far, we've covered what AI actually is (a general descriptor for machine learning, deep learning algorithms, and more) and how it differs from normal programs. We've also talked about a recap of what considerations you should keep in mind when coming up with AI-based solutions to problems/research questions you may find in the clinical setting. All of this information can likely be found in any other article or book; however, we're actually going to start applying the principles learned about in this chapter throughout the rest of this book.

The Rest of the Book…

As mentioned before, this book is not going to leave you with a general, vague, or "buzzword"-y understanding of AI. You'll actually be coding it, and that is going to require you to slog through some introductory and high-level material that may not immediately relate to AI in general; however, that material will be useful when thinking about how to program, implement, or adapt AI technologies for the problems you aim to solve.

Accordingly, the next chapter of this book is going to focus on the first step in this pathway: computational thinking. Specifically, that chapter will focus on algorithms, analysis of algorithms, and a general overview of general topics in algorithmic research right now. That chapter comprises a few examples that will illustrate how seemingly difficult problems can actually be solved quickly with a unique insight into the problem at hand. We will cover two main examples of problems that entail the use of algorithms: stable matching and activity selection. These algorithms themselves do not hold a particular relevance to the world of AI; however, they do serve to illustrate the topics of computational complexity, runtime analysis, and proof of correctness that will come up later in the book. Furthermore, they will start to hint at the general structure of thinking through problems computationally, showing that it is necessary to devise concrete, discrete, and detailed procedures to solve problems in a provably correct manner.

In the following chapter, we will dive into the world of programming, exposing you to concepts that are critical to structuring, writing, and running programs. In that chapter, we will implement a quadratic formula root finder. Though the example seems a little bit contrived, concepts such as variables, functions, and classes will be covered (which will also show up in later chapters). Additionally, we will implement a way to input .csv files containing a list of quadratic equations, giving us the opportunity to figure out how to work with file input and output. All of the earlier discussion will be done primarily in the Python programming language, which is the language of choice for beginners taking their first steps into programming and AI in general.

The chapter after that will take a break from the detour associated with establishing fundamental concepts of computer science and programming and, instead, focus on specific AI technologies and learning algorithms. This chapter, while not meant to be an exhaustive cover of all of the topics in AI, is meant to give an overview of salient and important algorithms that beginners should be able to understand at a high level. The mathematical proofs behind why these algorithms actually work will be left out (there are several books and online courses on this topic). Rather we will be focusing on what those mathematical proofs actually mean for the training, testing, and validation process of the AI algorithms we cover.

The two chapters after that will cover projects, built from scratch, involving AI in medicine. Specifically, we will code a machine learning pipeline to predict emergency room admissions from a dataset of basketball injuries, and we will then make deep neural networks that can predict pneumonia from chest x-rays. We will walk through the code for each of these examples and construct it, piece by piece, giving you an intuition and sense of the amount of work required to implement and adapt these AI technologies to solve problems at hand.

The last chapter will focus on the implications of AI in medicine. Mainly, we will talk about the potential use cases and misperceptions of AI in the medical field. Here, we will discuss patient data privacy and HIPAA and tales of AI snake oil in medicine (and how to spot telltale signs of fake AI products). We'll also discuss how to continue learning on your own and how to tackle a common task you'll face as a future programmer: fixing errors.

With all that being said, let's move on to Chapter 2.

CHAPTER 2

Computational Thinking

So far, we have been speaking about computers anthropomorphically, saying that they learn, carry out algorithms, etc. However, the only thing that a computer can actually do is follow a set list of instructions. In this chapter, we will be talking more about what that list of instructions should look like. We won't be getting into programming just yet, but we will be talking about "algorithmic thinking," that is, how to formulate steps of a solution for a program to execute. During this time, we'll also touch upon some theoretical problems with computation (including highlighting how some problems are highly inefficient to solve), how to determine the complexity of our algorithms (so we can try to work toward simpler solutions), and some algorithms/classes of algorithms that can offer alternatives to throwing an AI at your potential problem. A lot of this chapter will feel highly theoretical (because it is meant to be theoretical) and detached from AI, but does provide the underpinnings for starting to think like how a computer "thinks" (which is critical to learning how to program in general and program AI algorithms). With that disclaimer out of the way, let's talk about how computers actually work.

© Abhinav Suri 2022
A. Suri, *Practical AI for Healthcare Professionals*,
https://doi.org/10.1007/978-1-4842-7780-5_2

How Computers "Think"

At its most fundamental level, a computer operates in terms of binary numbers (i.e., 0s and 1s). From the perspective of an everyday programmer, it is unnecessary to really think about these numbers; however, it does get across the point that computers think in terms of numerical operations. The bare minimum set of computer operations supported by CPUs (central processing units) are variants of addition, multiplication, division, and loading/storing values from/in memory. However, given the incredible speed at which a computer operates, we can use these operations to get more complicated behaviors, such as the ability to compare two numbers, the ability to execute the same set of instructions multiple times, or even send information to an output device (such as a screen which will change the color of pixels based on values that are stored at a specific set of locations, called addresses, in computer memory).

Now, what does all of this mean for the beginning programmer? It means that computers are "dumb." They will do whatever you tell them to and very quickly; however, a computer will not be able to do anything that you want it to without you specifying the exact steps to do so. For example, in our BMI calculator example from earlier, the outline of what our program would do (i.e., take in two numbers, calculate a BMI, and spit out what weight category someone belongs to) is great from a conceptual perspective; however, it does not specify some additional behaviors. First of all, how are we accepting the individual input values? Additionally, how are we reporting back the actual weight category? Are we reading/writing those values to and from a file? At a higher level, how will a user utilize this function? Would we want them to interact with the tool via a website? If so, do we want to store prior calculations for easy reference?

All of the earlier questions, and more, are something that should be on your mind as you're working through defining a problem to solve. At its most basic level, a program has some form of input, a set of steps it does with that input, and an output. It is up to you to outline specifically what happens at each of those steps. If we were to reframe our BMI problem in the computational mindset, I would say that the input of the program is variable; however, for simplicity sake, we will make a tool available on a website. From there, the website will have two input boxes on the page: one for inputting the weight and another for inputting the height of the patient. When the user presses a separate button on the web page, a calculation will be executed to calculate a patient's BMI and report back a weight category. The results of the calculation will show up on the website for the user to see. One critical component I left out is exactly where the calculation takes place. There are actually two options for websites. The calculation can either take place on the web server which sent you the code for the page of the website you are viewing (which your web browser then interpreted and displayed for you), or the calculation can take place on the web page itself (i.e., within the browser) without contacting the server. Regardless of the details mentioned here, it should be evident that defining a problem and solution for a program can be rather complex.

At a higher level, when we talk about problems that can be solved with AI, we have to think of additional questions. First, how do we get enough training data for the AI algorithm they are choosing? What is the goal of that AI algorithm? What algorithm would be best for the task? How do we quantify how "wrong" an AI is? How do we test the efficacy of the algorithm after it has been trained?

In the case of an AI that aims to potentially detect tumors in MRI scans, we would need to have annotated MRI images from radiologists who manually mark the images and delineate the exact voxel location of the tumor (i.e., segment the tumor itself). Other questions arise from this task: what will the radiologists be using to annotate the imaging sequences, how does that program output segmentations, and is it easily readable by whatever program we are constructing? In the case that only a few radiologists create individual segmentations for a few MRI series, how can we augment the training set (i.e., apply image transformations to the data such as warping, scaling, cropping, brightening, etc.) to provide more data to the algorithm we are using?

Once we solidify how we are providing training data to the algorithm, another question we must ask is how will the algorithm be evaluated? Are we only evaluating the AI based on its ability to detect if *a* tumor is present in the image, or are more granular results desired? Is it necessary to classify what type of tumor is in the image, or is it enough to only report that there *might* be a tumor in an imaging study and mark it for further human analysis? The earlier questions will inform what measures we use to evaluate the AI and how "wrong" it is throughout its training process (and eventually while evaluating the program itself). Lastly, we need to determine how the input and output to the AI program will be accomplished and where it would be available (i.e. would it be located on an individual's computer or on a server?).

Once you have actually formatted your question or proposed procedure in terms of something that can be thought of from a computational perspective, the next question to ask is whether something is computationally feasible to solve or not.

What "Can" and "Cannot" Be Solved

While computers are incredibly fast at performing individual operations, there are some tasks that are infeasible to solve with traditional algorithmic methods. Being able to spot exactly which problems are infeasible is critical to learning how to craft research proposals and potential solutions for problems in the medical field.

From a formal perspective, computational infeasibility is defined as a problem that is indeed computable, but incredibly resource intensive to the point that it is not practical for a computer to carry out a task due to the amount of resources that would be required. One such example of a problem that is considered computationally infeasible is the traveling salesman problem (TSP). The problem is as follows: given a list of cities and distances between each pair of cities, what is the shortest possible route that visits each city exactly once and returns to the original city?

A first attempt at solution for this would be to pick one city. From there, pick one of the remaining cities and add that to a running total of the distance traveled. Once you have visited all cities at least once, then return back to the original city. The issue is that we need to find the shortest possible route. Our solution only offers one potential way to do this: try out every possible combination of city paths in order to find one that is the smallest possible distance. However, this operation could quickly become very complex. If we had four cities that were all equidistant from each other (i.e., four points arranged in a square), we would have four possible choices for our starting city, three choices for the city to travel to next, two after that, and one after that. This means that we would need to check 24 (4*3*2*1) distinct combinations of paths and find which one is the shortest.

Checking this relatively small number of paths is pretty small. However, what happens if we change the amount of cities we need to visit? As a general rule, we can see that our current algorithm requires us to check $n!$ different paths, where n is the number of cities. What if we change the number of cities to 100? Well, 100! is 9.3*10^157. That is an incomprehensibly large number and certainly more than what your single processor can do (which most likely executes 2*10^9 operations in a second). Some back of the envelope calculations means that it will take (at minimum) 10^138 years for us to check all the possible solutions. For some context, the heat death of the universe is expected to occur in 10^100 years, and at that point, our program would still be running. The approach we outlined is often called a "brute-force" approach because we are checking every single possible solution. Though the algorithm itself is relatively simple to understand, the amount of operations we need to do is simply too large to be feasible.

Of course, we can relax some of the constraints around this problem to enable us to solve something a little bit simpler. Instead of finding the shortest path, we could instead find a path that is generally considered to be "good enough" by iteratively picking the closest city we haven't visited yet. We will have no real guarantee that it will be the shortest path since we did not check all the possible solutions, but if you want a solution to a 100-city TSP problem before the heat death of the universe, you might be willing to consider using this algorithm (also called a "greedy algorithm" because of the fact that it immediately chooses the lowest-cost – i.e., smallest distance – path at each step).

Let's try another problem that is a bit simpler: trying to find a business in a phone book. An initial solution would be to painstakingly check each page in the phone book by flipping through the pages by hand. Well, no one really does this. We usually have some sort of heuristic (shortcut) in mind when we think about doing this task: flip to a page roughly in the vicinity where that name would be in the phone book. If it isn't on that page, determine if it will be before or after the page you flipped to. From there, repeat that procedure, resetting the bounds of the pages you are selecting from. Putting hard numbers to the situation, let's say a phone book has 500 pages and you need to find a business starting with "J." First, open the book to page 250. Let's say that businesses of the letter "O" are on that page, so we know that "J" businesses would be before that. Let's then pick the middle page from the range 0 to 250 instead of 0 to 500, say, page 125. Page 125 contains businesses with the name "H." So now we know that "J" businesses will come after page 125 and definitely before page 250. So let's pick the middle page in that range (around page 313), and we might find our business on that page!

Effectively this approach (called "recursion") is focused on breaking down a larger problem into smaller ones (called "subproblems") and then repeating the same operation on each of the subproblems until some point that we are considered done. Our procedure is basically the following: Given a set of things to look for that we know are ordered (the phone book in our case which we know is alphabetically ordered), pick the middle element. If that element is before the item we want to find, repeat the first step but on the second half of the set. If the element is after the item we want to find, repeat the previous procedure but on the first half of the set. Once we find the desired element, stop and report back results. If our phone book has just eight pages, it is actually provable that, in the worst case, we can find the page our desired business is on in just three iterations. Here, the worst case would be that our business is on the first (or last page) of the phone book (so we would open to page 4, then go to 2, then go to 1, and finish). Generalizing this rule, if we had n elements to search, we would find the desired element in $log_2(n)$ iterations of the algorithm. The fact that this is operating on a logarithmic scale is great because if our phone book had 2048 pages, we would only need to perform a flip (at maximum) 11 times!

The previous algorithms work to illustrate two extremes of potential problems one might face while approaching solving an issue. On one hand, you might come across a solution that takes an incredibly long time to solve, leading you to either limit the size of the problem (in our case, limiting the amount of cities to something much smaller than 100) or loosen constraints so you can get a solution that works with computational restraints (i.e., pursue the "good enough" greedy approach). On the other hand, you might get a problem that works really well at almost all scales (i.e., our "recursive" solution) with a little bit of intuitive thinking.

Now, how does all of this relate to AI in general? Think back to our traveling salesman problem (TSP). We know that if we had n cities, we would need to check $n!$ different potential solutions to find the one that yields the shortest potential path. We would designate this algorithm as being non-polynomial where "polynomial" would indicate that the function is less than an expression n^k (where n is the size of the input and k is some constant that is not a variable; note, we also ignore any constants and assume that we are only evaluating the "less than" expression only past some general constant). $n!$ can only be upper bounded by a function n^n, and since the exponent n is not a constant and changes with the size of the input, it is not polynomial. Such problems fall into the general class known as "NP-Hard" because (very, very, very roughly) it is thought that they cannot be solved in polynomial time (but the jury is still out on that). Deep learning algorithms fall into the realm of NP-Hard problems and share similar solving times seen in the traveling salesman problem (i.e., not polynomial time).

More on complexity classes   There are also other complexity classes that exist. The phone book search problem (formally called binary search) is one that can be solved in polynomial time (upper bounded by n) and belongs to the complexity class "P." "NP" problems are ones that can have their solutions verified in polynomial time. In terms of TSP, if we changed the constraint from "find the shortest path" to "find a path of length less than X," then it is really easy to check if a solution is correct (just add up the lengths of the hops between the cities rather than try out all possible paths and if the proposed one is the same as the shortest path among all possibilities). "NP-Hard" problems more accurately problems that are *at least* as hard as problems in NP (i.e., a problem in NP could be "rephrased" as an NP-Hard problem), and "NP-Complete" problems are ones that are both "NP" and "NP-Hard." An issue that is talked about in computer science is whether P = NP or not. It is essentially asking whether a problem that has a solution that can be verified in polynomial time has a way to find that solution in polynomial time.

Of course, ML, DL, and AI algorithms have various looser constraints and shortcuts they take to try to come to a solution that is "good enough" for most cases. For instance, instead of trying to find the optimal way to produce the correct outputs, some AI algorithms tend to leave the judgment of "good enough" up to the user and ask for a prespecified limit on how long it takes to train the network. Accordingly, it is incredibly rare to find an algorithm that can operate at 100% accuracy all the time (and if someone purports to find one that is 100% accurate, you should be suspicious). But overall, AI problems are ones that have a higher computational complexity and thus take a longer time to solve. This brings means that AI algorithms sometimes require a fair amount of computation to train (e.g., Google spends thousands of dollars training its natural language processing models) and creators of these programs need to be cognizant of the potential resource constraints induced by the NP-Hard nature of AI.

Now that we've covered a computational view of what can and cannot be solved, I would be remiss not to mention that there are other reasons why it would be impossible to solve certain problems in the world of AI. These primarily deal with practical constraints of the tools you have available to you. For example, if you want to make a way to track steps for patients using their mobile phone, one of the things you have to make sure of is that the phone that your patients are using has an accelerometer (measures tilt of a phone) that you can access the readings of, or the phone itself has some way to access the amount of steps a person has taken that day (e.g., Apple devices allow app developers to access step data and heart rate information for users that have an iPhone or Apple Watch). If you don't have the right tools available to you, a problem can easily become one that is infeasible, so definitely make sure that you are approaching the problem that is aimed to solve correctly.

Algorithmic Alternatives

As we covered in the prior section, non-AI algorithms can potentially yield efficient solutions and several already have done so in the realm of healthcare. Here we will cover some of the types of non-AI based algorithmic alternatives that exist. The title of this section is somewhat of a misnomer as there is not necessarily a single list of algorithms or class of algorithms that can solve a problem you might be facing. However, I will make an attempt to illustrate a couple of examples of utilizations of algorithms in healthcare and biology. By no means are these examples meant to be comprehensive; rather they aim to show that throwing AI at a particular problem might not be the best solution to all given issues one may face in the world of healthcare. With that disclaimer out of the way, let's look at an algorithm that several readers may be familiar with.

Stable Matching

If you are a physician in the United States, one algorithm you may have interacted with during your training is the Gale-Shapley stable matching algorithm. This algorithm (with a few alterations) determines what hospitals and specialties applicants will spend the next several years at while pursuing their residency. However, the idea behind the algorithm originates from a simpler problem: finding optimal marriages.

The underpinning of the matching algorithm starts with a theoretical situation. Let's say there are some men and some women (equal numbers in each group), each with preferences about who they would want to eventually marry (men draw up a ranked proposal list, women draw up a ranked acceptance list). The goal of this algorithm is to create a *stable matching* which is a pairing of all men and women such that no pair of a man M and a woman W exists where M and W prefer each other over the people they are eventually matched to. Practically, it means that the goal of this algorithm is to prevent eloping (i.e., if everything goes well, we will know that someone did not get their first preference because the first preference rejected that person). Achieving this guarantee of providing a stable matching is important, since (in the real world) we want to make sure that all of the residents and hospitals get the residents that they actually want (and not have the situation where a better resident-hospital pair was possible but did not happen).

So how do we solve this problem? One attempt would be to list out every possible matching of men and women and then check to see which ones are stable. Doing so would give us a list of all possible stable matchings; however, it would also be very computationally expensive. To explore how computationally expensive it is, imagine we have three men and three women. Enumerating all possibilities would yield six possible distinct matchings (prove this for yourself if you want) which is not too bad. But more generally, this strategy would require you to list out $n!$ different matches (if we have n men and n women) and then check to see which ones are actually stable. Generating a factorial number of matches can be very computationally expensive even at small numbers of n (e.g., 20! is 2.43e18) and certainly not feasible to handle the thousands of medical students who apply every year to residencies.

In 1962, David Gale and Lloyd Shapely proposed a solution that could solve the stable matching problem and do so in something on the order of n^2 operations. Their solution is the following.

If there is someone who is not engaged yet, do the following:

- Each unengaged man should propose to the woman he prefers the most as long as he has not proposed to that woman before.

- Each unmatched woman temporarily "engages" to the man whom she has ranked the highest among the proposals she receives. If she is matched but receives an offer of engagement from a man she ranks higher than the one she is currently "engaged" to, she will leave that man and engage to the new man (i.e., she trades up).

This process repeats until everyone is engaged to someone (if there is a match between the number of men and women). The algorithm guarantees that everyone has to be engaged and that all the engagements (soon to be marriages) are stable. To prove the latter point, imagine that a man, Mike, and a woman, Wendy, liked each other, but did not end up engaged in the end (Mike ended up engaged to Alice and Wendy engaged to Bob). They are confused as to how this is a possibility. However, per the algorithm, we know that Wendy must have rejected Mike at some point (either when she was free or when she was temporarily engaged) in favor of Bob. In the end, we know that there cannot be an instability in matching because one party must have rejected the other party at some point in favor of a higher preference.

This algorithm is notably faster than the initial permutation approach (i.e., listing out all possible matchings and checking for stability). But it does not guarantee that we get the most optimal matching since the word "optimal" depends on whose perspective you are taking. The Gale-Shapley algorithm can be constructed to favor men over women or women over men (the one mentioned earlier gives first choice for the man and thus ensures that they get the best possible outcome). Regardless, the ideas behind the stable matching problem play a role in the national Residency Matching Program with alterations to account for the fact that there are more medical students applying than hospitals available, different multiple residency positions for hospitals (one side can have multiple engagements), and couples who would prefer to match into the same hospital or city but with different specialties. Accounting for couples in the matching algorithm actually makes the problem NP-complete. Stable matching algorithms hold relevance beyond the world of residency matching and are most notably used in the process of determining the dynamics of organ exchanges, allocating donor-acceptor pairs for critical kidney surgeries when next of kin are incompatible with the patient in need of a transplant.

Notably, using this traditional algorithm, we did not need to involve the usage of AI techniques in any way. There was no need to train a neural network on prior examples of stable matchings and no way to train an algorithm to produce a correct matching. We simply set out a prescribed set of instructions and proved that those instructions would lead to the outcome we wanted. If we were to make an AI based solution to this, we would have a much higher time complexity than the Gale-Shapeley algorithm, and we would not have the guarantee of producing optimal matchings (since AI algorithms rarely reach 100% accuracy). Here, the non-AI algorithm beats the AI approach in all metrics.

Activity Selection

Another algorithm that can come in handy in healthcare is the activity selection algorithm. Imagine you are in charge of a clinic and have to schedule physicians so that they see a set of patients you have already booked for specific time slots in an optimal manner. Some of these time slots overlap. Additionally, these patients, for the purposes of this problem, do not have a preference for which physician they see, but do have appointments that differ in length. So effectively, you have a list of start and end times and are trying to figure out what is the best possible way that you can allocate a physician to see the maximum number of patients in a given time period.

Formally, we can think of the appointment times of patients as a set of individual items. Each item contains two attributes that describe it. In our case, those attributes are the start time of the appointment and the end time of the appointment. Effectively, our goal is to find the largest set such that all the individual items in the sets do not overlap with respect to their start and end times (as a violation of that constraint would mean we are scheduling a doctor to be in two places at once, which is not possible).

So how do we come up with a solution to this problem? One particularly brute force solution is to list out all of the possibilities of sets, filter out the ones that do not contain appointments that are compatible with each other (i.e., they overlap and cause the doctor to be scheduled for two places at once), and then find the largest sized set among these.

But let's think about how long it would take to construct such a set. Well, this is actually equivalent to 2^n where n denotes the size of the set of appointments. As an example, if we just had three appointments in our set (named a, b, and c), we could make the following sets (where {...} denotes a distinct set): {}, {a}, {b}, {c}, {a, b}, {b, c}, {c, a}, {a, b, c} = 8 = 2^3 sets (note, we include the set with no elements since it is possible to schedule a doctor with no appointments for that day). This is formally called the power set.

Side Note   Proving a power set contains 2^n elements. We can formally prove that a set of n elements constructs a power set of 2^n elements by a process known as induction. The intuition behind induction is to establish logic stating that if some assumption regarding a subset of the problem is taken as true, then, if we continue that logic for a slightly larger subset of the problem and show we get expected results, the assumption will generally hold. Formally, we can make an induction hypothesis for our case that says the following: "Assume that if we have k elements in a set (where $k \geq 1$), there will be 2^k elements in its power set. Then if we have $k + 1$ elements in the set, we need to show that there will be 2^{k+1} elements in the power set. We can show this by saying that in the $k+1$ case, each element of the power set has two copies, one containing the $k+1^{th}$ element and the other being the original copy. This gives us $2^k + 2^k = 2 * 2^k = 2^{k+1}$ elements, showing our induction hypothesis holds true when we make the problem slightly larger (this is formally called the induction step). When $k = n - 1$, we can use our induction hypothesis to say that the set containing $k + 1 = n$ elements would have $2^{k+1} = 2^{(n-1)+1} = 2^n$ elements. There's also one bit of the induction proof I left out called the "base case," but that is just stating what happens when $k = 0$ since those are special cases (we have to confirm that the definition holds for something called the "empty set").

So if we are constructing a power set every time we want to solve this problem, we are effectively creating a problem that takes an exponential amount of operations (i.e., the number of sets we need to construct) to even begin to solve. As we've covered before, for a small number of operations, this is feasible (e.g., for three appointments, we only need to make eight sets to check). However, for something like 20 patients in a day, we would need to make over 1 million sets (1,048,576). On top of that, we would need to check each set to see which elements are overlapping or not.

However, we can adopt a "greedy" mindset toward this problem where we focus on making a lot of locally optimal choices to get to a final, globally optimal solution. What do I mean by that? Well, in this case, it means we don't have to worry about choosing the optimal set of appointments that maximizes the number of patients a physician sees. Rather, we're just going to iteratively make choices at various steps at the problem without regard for their future consequence. What might that greedy solution look like in our case? Well, if we're starting off with the set of appointments for the day, one approach might be to add the patient whose appointment finishes earliest in the day and add that to our growing set of patients to see. To pick the next patient, we'll then just pick the next patient whose appointment time period does not overlap with the first patient's appointment, but does finish earliest among the remaining patients. If we keep on doing this, we may eventually construct our optimal set.

Okay, so what would be the operational time required to do this? Well, we would need to search through all of the set for the appointment that finishes earliest. In the worst case, that appointment would be located at the end of the list, and we would need to look through n items to find it. Adding that appointment into our final set and checking if it conflicts with some other appointment takes a negligible amount of time. When we go to pick the new potential appointment to add into our set, we then search for the next appointment that starts after the appointment we have just scheduled. This would require us to look through $n - 1$ different appointments and so on. Overall, we would need to search approximately $\frac{n(n-1)}{2}$ appointments, which is fine, but could use some improvement. However, if we were to sort these appointments by their finish time in ascending order initially, we could get a speed up during the process of finding the earliest compatible appointment among the ones left in the main set. The initial amount of operations associated with sorting the set is somewhat high (actually this is something on the order of $n * log(n)$), but it will actually require less operations than before whenever n is large. So that gives us a little bit of optimization in our problem, but how do we show that our solution is actually optimal and gets us what we actually wanted. After all, when we think of "greedy" things, we tend to think about a lot of shortsighted decisions that lead to bad outcomes in the end. Well, in our case, we can actually prove that being greedy, sometimes, is good.

We can do so by proving two properties of our approach: (1) a greedy-choice property, defined as the fact that a global optimal solution can be found by making locally optimal greedy choices, and (2) the optimal substructure property, defined as the fact that an optimal solution is comprised of optimal subparts. Let's set out to prove that our approach satisfies these two properties.

To prove the first property, it is sufficient to show that if there is an optimal solution to this problem, it always contains the first patient in our sorted set of appointments (i.e., it begins with the patient whose appointment finishes the earliest) called p. To see why, suppose there exists some optimal set of appointments that doesn't start with the appointment p (call this set B) and another set that does (A). We can show that any optimal set can be constructed so that it starts with the first appointment as follows: remove the non-p appointment and replace it with p. We can do this operation because we know that p will not overlap with anything in B that exists right now. The number of appointments in A and B is the same, but we have shown that any optimal solution can start with the greedy choice.

Great, but if we're starting off with the greedy choice, how does that prove that successively making greedy choices leads to the optimal solution? We do so by proving optimal substructure. Let's start with a general conjecture. If a set A is a solution to the appointment problem for the entire set of appointments, then a solution that omits appointment p from A (call this set A') will be the optimal solution to the appointment problem that does not contain the p appointment. This conjecture is basically saying if we have an optimal solution and take a subset of a problem, the optimal solution to that subset will be contained within the globally optimal solution.

How do we prove this? We can use a technique called proof by contradiction. Our goal will be to prove that a statement S is true by somehow showing that the opposite of S is not possible by showing an internal contradiction to some principle (thereby showing that S being true is the only possibility). In our case, our statement S is that A' is the optimal solution for the case when our set of appointments omits p. So the opposite of our statement is that there is some other set (call this B') that contains more elements than A'. So, if we then add p back into the set of appointments to pick from, an optimal solution should contain that appointment. If we add p to B' and call this new set of appointments B, we construct a set of optimal solutions to the problem that is actually larger than A, which we assumed to be the optimal solution earlier. We have arrived at a contradiction, which indicates that the set B' cannot exist and that the set A that was constructed is truly optimal and A' is an optimal solution to the subproblem not containing appointment p. We can extend this logic to continue making greedy choices to solve smaller and smaller subproblems (the solutions of which are also optimal), to ultimately show that we can construct the globally optimal solution.

Well, that was a lot to take in, but it does indicate some ideas that are important. Algorithms are provably correct, they run in a deterministic fashion, and they can yield enormous benefits over a brute-force approach. When we think about this problem in terms of AI, once again, we would have to find some way to train an AI model to come up with this logic (which is already difficult to do), and even then, we have no particular guarantee that it will work in all cases (since AI is very much a black box: i.e., it is difficult to determine exactly how the AI has come up with the solution it has). In the case of our activity selection problem, the greedy approach is the best one.

Analysis of Algorithms and Other Algorithms

Some of the explanations earlier included mentions of the number of operations, amount of time it would take something to occur, etc. However, computer scientists are rarely concerned with counting up the number of individual operations involved with a particular algorithm. Rather they are more interested in what the general order of magnitude of operations executed is (i.e., 10s, 100s, 1000s, 1000000s, etc.). But not all operations are considered equal. For instance, the act of assigning and keeping track of a values is considered to be almost negligible. There also is not any consideration for how long it would take to access files from the system, download information, wait for user input, etc. The only components of an algorithm that matter (when doing algorithmic analysis) are the ones that actually incur some degree of cost to them, that is, repetitive operations, such as searching for values in a list of numbers. Furthermore, in the analysis of algorithms, we don't consider the speed of one computer over another and just assume that there is a base unit of a "time step" which holds no real-life meaning (but is meant to allow comparisons between algorithms).

So this model, formally called the RAM (Random Access Memory) model of computation, basically is assuming you have some theoretical computer that is not really concerned with real-life constraints. The advantage of this assumption is that we do not have to concern ourselves with the performance of hardware, etc., when determining how good our algorithm is. The disadvantage is that the number of time steps we analyze our algorithm would need to operate does not equate to real-world time.

For example, we were looking at the program for determining if someone is obese or not, that algorithm would take one time step to perform the division operation and set it equal to a variable, one time step to evaluate each comparison operation, and one another time step to output the result. In the worst case, that would lead us to take five comparisons (i.e., we evaluate all the prior comparisons before getting to the last one). Counting up all of the time steps for this problem is easy, but what about our activity selection problem? That gets a little bit more complicated. But what we can do is analyze the pseudocode (i.e., not actual code, but code that is written to convey semantic meaning) of the algorithm and find the resulting time required at each step.

Activity Selection (set of appointments):

```
    S = Sort (set of appointments) by finish time

    Optimal Set = {First Element in S}

    For each element e in S after the 1st element
    do the following:
            If the start time of the eth appointment
            is after the most recently added element
            in Optimal Set:
                    Add the eth appointment to the
                    Optimal Set.
    Output the Optimal Set
```

A little item of note: The first line of the pseudocode is a **function header**. It specifies the name of the function that we are running (in this case "activity selection") and a list of **parameters** needed for the function to run in parenthesis immediately following that name (in this case the set of appointments we're going to perform the operation on). Additionally, the "=" sign here does not mean equality, rather it means assignment (e.g. if I say "x = 5" I am assigning the value "5" to the variable "x").

Let's actually start by taking a look at the part starting with "for." Each of the operations is as follows: a comparison check and adding something to a set. Both of the operations will take one time step to do. If the number of activities we are dealing with is n, then it would take at maximum $2n$ operations to go through the entire set and construct the optimal set (and that is assuming that all of the appointments are spaced out such that none overlap with each other and the optimal set is equivalent to the original set of appointments). We can express this in the form of something called "Big O" notation. We are going to drop the constant in front of this term and just say that this part of the program will take $O(n)$ time to do it. Formally, saying that $2n = O(n)$ means that there exist some constants c and k such that $0 \leq 2n \leq c * n$ for all $n \geq k$. In this case, c would be 2 and k would be 0. Another example of Big O notation would be saying that $n^2 + n + 1 = O(n^2)$. Essentially, we only care about the largest magnitude term in our expression for the amount of operations an algorithm takes. In the $n^2 + n + 1$ example, for a large enough n, it really does not matter how large the $n + 1$ part is going to be. The n^2 term of the algorithm will always be the largest contributor to the **runtime** (i.e., approximately how long it would take an algorithm to run in terms of time steps) of the algorithm.

So our algorithm could be considered to be $O(n)$ for that part. But what about the other major operation that we have consolidated into a single line, the "sort" operation. That itself actually contains a number of other distinct operations I have collapsed, but those operations run in $O(n \log n)$ time. So the total time for the algorithm is $O(n \log n) + O(n)$. But that time could be simplified even further to $O(n \log n)$ alone since; at large values of n, the contribution of the linear portion of the algorithm will not take a lot of time to do in comparison to the linearithmic ($O(n \log n)$) portion.

Over topics and types of algorithms that might be useful to you at some point are as follows:

- **Sorting Algorithms**: As the name would imply, these algorithms are in charge of helping you find the fastest way to sort information in a particular order. There is a theoretical "best" time we can get for sorting algorithms and that is $O(n \log n)$, *but* this time bound only applies for comparison-based sorting methods (which means that we only can sort based on comparing two objects at a time). However, non-comparison-based sorting algorithms (which take into account properties of things like digits in the case of numerical data) can run in linear time (i.e., quicker than comparison-based sorting algorithms).

- **Graph Algorithms**: Graph algorithms are concerned with trying to find ways to do operations on nodes (think of these as items) and edges (think of these as connections between the items). Our stable marriage problem was a variant of a graph algorithm problem in a certain aspect (more generally, this is known as the stable matching problem; nodes = men and women, marriage = edge connection). Finding mutual friends on Facebook is a problem that can be solved with graph algorithms. Think of yourself as a node that is connected to current friends (i.e., other nodes) by edges. Mutual friends would be individuals who are connected by an edge to your friends as well. We can use algorithms to make the computational cost associated with finding all your mutual friends as efficient as possible.

- **Dynamic Programming**: This is a more advanced topic, but effectively boils down to trying to cut down on computation time by reusing computations you have done before to help you find an optimal solution. An example would be finding the some nth Fibonacci number. One solution would be to calculate all the Fibonacci numbers up until n; however, we would waste a lot of calculation time since the definition for Fibonacci numbers relies on you knowing the prior two Fibonacci numbers (and calculating those would require more time and so on). We can instead store the result of the Fibonacci numbers below the *nth* one so we do not have to redo this computation. Taking a dynamic programming approach to this particular problem yields an $O(n)$ runtime (much better than the $O(2^n)$ runtime for the naïve solution.

- **Approximation Algorithms**: While our prior algorithms have been concerned with trying to find the optimal solution to all of the problems we encounter, this class of algorithms tries to find a solution that is "good enough." It is useful to relax the constraints on our solutions, especially for computationally intractable problems. Importantly, this class of algorithms still tries to give guarantees of how "off" the solution is in its worst case which is useful.

- **String Algorithms**: Are primarily concerned with performing operations on strings which are sequences of letters (and sometimes numbers). For example, "word" is a string and "ACTGA" is also a string. The field of bioinformatics is especially involved with string algorithms which can help determine the phylogeny of species based on how similar their DNA is. Some of the algorithms in this class of algorithms relate a lot to other classes (e.g., an algorithm known as the "Longest Common Subsequence" algorithm can help find similar subsequences of DNA between two genetic samples).

- **Data Structures**: This topic is concerned with structuring and storing information/data in the aforementioned algorithms to optimize for operations like search, insert, update, edit, and deletion times. For example, if we were keeping track of 1000s of patients and wanted to be able to search for various characteristics about them, how would we structure the data to enable fast search times? We would probably want to keep our information sorted by a particular parameter, but how would that sorted data structure work and what happens when we add in a new patient (how long would it take to return to a sorted state upon adding the new information)? Some data structures that are commonly mentioned are trees (which structure data so that each element in a tree may be connected to some "parent" node and has some number of "children" nodes, similar to a phylogeny tree), hash tables (which help index data into a form where lookup times are instantaneous, eliminating the need to search through an entire dataset for a particular value), stacks (where information is added in a particular manner to optimize access time for most or least recently added elements depending on construction), and queues (where elements are "connected" to each other in an ordered manner similar to a line).

All of the previous information may or may not be useful to you as you consider potential AI solutions to whatever healthcare problems you face. However, the purpose of this book is to give you a lay of the land and enough knowledge of the terminology to take on a learning path of your own. Knowledge of algorithms and data structures can help take seemingly difficult or computationally complex problems into the realm of simple and very quick to run if you have enough knowledge about the existing algorithms out there. Before considering whether a potential solution truly needs AI, think about the critical information in your problem statement. Then determine whether the operation can be boiled down to an algorithmic problem (that can be solved in a deterministic way) or if you would need an AI to "learn" how to solve particular problems that are difficult to delineate the parameters of entirely.

Conclusion

The primary purpose of this chapter was to start to give you some idea as to the role of thinking from a computational perspective. The topics mentioned are somewhat sparse (and could easily take an entire book to cover completely), but alas we must move on to concepts that can get you to the point that you can start to program the algorithms that were mentioned earlier. In the next chapter, we're going to take a step beyond writing theoretical pseudocode and actually make your first program using a computer coding language known as Python. This exercise will give you the opportunity to learn programming, which is required for you to create AI programs.

CHAPTER 3

Overview of Programming

Now that we have covered some of the basics of computer science and algorithms, it's time to get into the nitty-gritty of applying those concepts. Just as an astronomer uses a telescope to carry out their craft, so does the computer scientist using programming to bring their algorithms and ideas into reality. The point is that programming is a tool for transforming procedural steps into real life code that can be used. Consequently, we need to understand how to write these programs so that we can get actually useful outputs from an algorithm or (in the coming chapters) an AI program. In this chapter, we'll be writing up a program to do a simple task, finding the roots of a quadratic equation. The task, though not clinically relevant, gives us the opportunity to explore several concepts in programming. First, we'll go over what programs are. Then, we'll outline the task at hand. Finally, we'll go through a few attempts at trying to solve the task at hand, learning basic Python syntax and concepts along the way.

But First, What Are Programs?

Programs themselves are just text files. Text files by themselves do not do anything. Rather we must feed those text files into a another program

---

All supporting code for this chapter can be found at `https://github.com/Apress/Practical-AI-for-Healthcare-Professionals/tree/main/ch3`

© Abhinav Suri 2022
A. Suri, *Practical AI for Healthcare Professionals*,
https://doi.org/10.1007/978-1-4842-7780-5_3

whose job is to *interpret* those text files, line by line, and produce useful output based on the syntax (arrangement of commands) present in that text file.

> **Side Note**: Sometimes, the programs that interpret text files may actually do something called *compiling*. A program that compiles something (a *compiler*) will translate that program into machine code (a.k.a. assembly language). This representation of your program is almost equivalent to the 1s and 0s that your computer processor (CPU) uses to execute instructions (i.e., steps) of your program. The big advantage of compiling something is that it should work on almost any machine and it will be very fast (since the program is already in a format that your CPU can understand). Programs that must be interpreted will require that the end user of your program have the interpreting program installed on their machines. There are exceptions to the rules (e.g., programs that interpret segments of code but compile other segments that are used often to save time), but this is the general dichotomy of programs that execute other programs.

But if programs are text files, how do we tell computers what exactly to do? It is pretty clear that you can't just type in "Diagnose this patient with X based on Y characteristics." Rather, programs must be written in a specific format (using some special words) to produce the expected output. There are many different ways to write up instructions in these formats, and each of those different ways is known as a language. There are several programming languages out there such as C, Python, R, Java, and much more. Each of them is optimized for a specific goal: C is generally considered to be used to make very efficient programs. Python is used for scientific computing. R tends to be used for statistics. Java tends to be used to create applications that can be used on any operating system (so long as they have Java installed). For this book, we will be learning how to use **Python** since it is used widely in research and scientific computing tasks involving machine learning and AI in general.

Getting Started with Python

In order to write Python, you do not need anything on your system other than a text editor (on Mac, this is TextEdit; on Windows, this is Notepad). However, in order to execute (a.k.a. "run") Python programs, you will need to have the Python interpreter installed on your computer. To make things simple (and to help ensure that all readers of this book have a similar experience), I would advise that you instead use Colab by Google. To get that running, go to `https://colab.research.google.com/`, and sign in with your google account.

Then go to the "File" menu (in the upper left-hand corner), and click "New Notebook." You should be greeted with a blank screen that just contains a single gray cell with a play button next to it (refer to Figure 3-1).

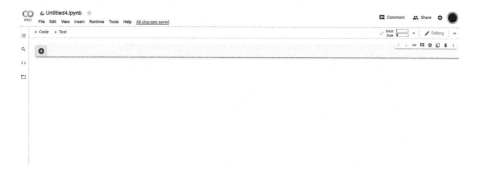

Figure 3-1. *This is what a blank Colab notebook should look like*

Side Note: In the case that Colab is not available when you are reading this book, you should do the following (note: the instructions cannot be too specific since standards for how to do the following vary as the years go by): 1) Download a Python installation for your system. 2) Create a folder in your system as the place where you will write your programs. 3) You will need to learn how to use the command line in your system. Look up a tutorial for this. For Windows, it is also advised that you enable Windows Subsystem for Linux. 4) Once you do that, open a terminal/command prompt, and type in "cd" followed by the path to the folder where you want to write your programs. For example, if that is on your desktop in a folder called "MyPrograms," I would write `cd ~/Desktop/MyPrograms`. Here, the ~ represents the path to the home directory. 5) With your Python installation, you should have something called "pip" installed (this is a package manager which allows you to download programs that other people have made). To verify that you have this installed, in your command prompt, type `python -m pip --version`, and you should get some output along the lines `pip X.Y.Z`. 6) Run `pip install notebook` in your command line. Note: it would be best to follow the instructions at `https://jupyter.org/install` to get the most up-to-date instructions for how to install Jupyter notebook on your computer using pip. 7) Run `jupyter notebook` and open the web browser.

This is not quite the text files I was talking about earlier. Rather it is a quick prototyping tool known as a notebook. In this setting, you can run single lines of programs without needing to worry about saving files and running things from the command line. This is optimal for creating programs that help in an exploratory analysis of data or creating one-off lines of code.

In the first cell (the thing with the gray block), type in the following:

```
print("Hello world")
```

Then click the play button on the left, or press Shift+Enter on your keyboard.

You should see the text "Hello world" printed out. Congratulations, you have written your first program!

What Just Happened?

The line print("Hello world") will execute a function called print that exists in the Python standard library. What is a function? A function is a set of code that takes in an input and usually produces some output (based on the input value). Several of simple functions are packaged with the Python language when you install it (i.e., the standard library). Others functions you will have to define yourself. The function print takes in a single input (called an argument). That input is just the text you would like to be output from the print function. Print will then copy that text (a.k.a. a "string") over to something called the "standard output." The standard output will display that text to you, the person executing the program. The standard output is not incredibly important to understand right now, but the concept to keep in mind is that a program can output its results directly to the screen.

Stepping It Up a Bit

Let's try and do something a little bit more complicated, like finding the roots of a quadratic formula. As a refresher from school, we know that if an equation has the general form of $ax^2 + bx + c$, it will have two solutions:

$$\frac{-b \pm \sqrt{b^2 - 4ac}}{2a}$$

Let's try an initial shot at how we might do this in Python for the equation $x^2 - 8x + 12$. Maybe we can just type in stuff as we do in a calculator.

Type in the following into the next cell (click the "+ Code" button if you don't have another cell available):

```
(-(-8) + ((-8)^2 - (4*1*12))^(1/2))/(2*1)
```

Then click run.

You should see something along these lines of

```
TypeError Traceback (most recent call last)
<ipython-input-4-f7fc0a4be28c> in <module>()
----> 1 (-(-8) + ((-8)^2 - (4*1*12))^(1/2))/(2*1)

TypeError: unsupported operand type(s) for ^: 'int' and 'float'
```

Since we aren't seeing our expected output and we see the word "Error" in the output, we can safely assume we did something wrong. Going to the last line of the output, we see that we have something called a "TypeError" and that we have an unsupported operand types for "^". What does this mean?

Well, it turns out that in Python, "^" does not raise something to the power of something else. Rather it actually does a bitwise exclusive OR on what is to the left and what is to the right of the carat (don't worry about what this exactly is).

After some searching, it turns out that you have to use ** when taking the power of something in Python. Let's try this again:

INPUT

```
(-(-8) + ((-8)**2 - (4*1*12))**(1/2))/(2*1)
```

OUTPUT

```
6.0
```

Great! And to get the other output, let's type in the cell the other form of the equation:

INPUT

```
(-(-8) + ((-8)**2 - (4*1*12))**(1/2))/(2*1)
(-(-8) - ((-8)**2 - (4*1*12))**(1/2))/(2*1)
```

OUTPUT

```
2.0
```

Hmm... so why are we only seeing one output this time? Well, this is just an oddity with Python notebooks. It will only print out the last line of a set of commands unless you explicitly print out a value before then. So let's just wrap both of our equations in a "print" function like so:

INPUT

```
print((-(-8) + ((-8)**2 - (4*1*12))**(1/2))/(2*1))
print((-(-8) - ((-8)**2 - (4*1*12))**(1/2))/(2*1))
```

OUTPUT

```
6.0
2.0
```

That's great! We get the outputs we expected, but what if someone asks us to get the roots of a different quadratic equation? What if they ask us to get the roots of 100 different quadratic equations? Well, we may be out of luck because we would need to somehow change our program for each of those inputs, unless there is some other solution out there.

Variables, Methods/Functions, String Operations, Print String Interpolation Applied

It turns out there is such a solution. We can store the values for a, b, and c into something called variables. Variables are just letters or words that can be assigned to some value. We can then just use the variables to carry out our calculations.

Redoing our expression in terms of variables, it would look something like the following:

INPUT

```
a = 1 # setting a equal to 1
b = -8 # setting b equal to -8
c = 12 # setting c equal to 12
print((-(b) + ((b)**2 - (4*a*c))**(1/2))/(2*a))
print((-(b) - ((b)**2 - (4*a*c))**(1/2))/(2*a))
```

OUTPUT

```
6.0
2.0
```

A couple of things to note about the earlier example. First, lines that have a # some text will not be interpreted past the # mark. They are used to "comment" code (i.e., leave a note for people reading the code later on). Second, when we write a = 1, we are setting the variable a equal to the value of 1. We can set variables equal to anything, even other variables!

When we rewrite our expression, we only need to rewrite the explicit numbers in our expression and can instead refer to them by their variables.

Also, it looks like the +/- part of our quadratic equation solver can be cleaned up a bit to not repeat our code (this is a process called "refactoring"). We can instead set the $\sqrt{b-4ac}$ part equal to another variable called sqrt_part.

INPUT

```
a = 1 # setting a equal to 1
b = -8 # setting b equal to -8
c = 12 # setting c equal to 12
sqrt_part = ((b)**2 - (4*a*c))**(1/2)
print((-(b) + sqrt_part)/(2*a))
print((-(b) - sqrt_part)/(2*a))
```

OUTPUT

```
6.0
2.0
```

Great, we still get our same outputs, and we have cleaned up the code a bit (it looks a bit less like a glob of variables and numbers).

> **Side Note**: Variables (e.g., a and sqrt_part) can be named anything, but there are some rules as to how they can be named. Typically, they cannot start with a number and cannot contain ?, #, +, -, <spaces>, ', or ", and they usually cannot be part of a set of "reserved words" (e.g., "print") which already refer to functions/syntax in the Python ecosystem. A safe bet would be to name your variables only using letters and an underscore _ to make variable names readable to humans.

But the issue still remains that we must manually specify what a, b, and c are. We can help solve that by making this code cell into a function. This function will accept text (a.k.a. a string) containing the quadratic formula we want to solve and output the two solutions.

To define a function (called a "method" in Python), we will wrap our code in that function and specify a single argument to that function (i.e., the string containing the quadratic formula):

```python
def root_finder(quadratic):
  a = 1 # setting a equal to 1
  b = -8 # setting b equal to -8
  c = 12 # setting c equal to 12
  sqrt_part = ((b)**2 - (4*a*c))**(1/2)
  print((-(b) + sqrt_part)/(2*a))
  print((-(b) - sqrt_part)/(2*a))
```

Note   In Python, we must "indent" the inner body of our function by pressing the "tab" character.

We can execute this function (i.e., "call" it) by writing `root_finder("some text")` in another cell. Right now, it will not actually interpret our text we input, but it will output the results from the previous quadratic we were working on so far.

To actually go from the text of a quadratic to getting the values of a, b, and c, we need to make some assumptions about how someone will input values into our function. Let's assume that someone will specify the quadratic as `"ax^2 + bx + c = 0"`. We can do the following to get the values we want:

1) "Split" the input string into three parts: one containing ax^2, another containing bx, and the last containing c. Those three parts are roughly split if we can remove the " + " part of the equation.

2) For the ax^2 part, remove the "x^2" part of our string and convert the "a" part into a number. For the bx part, remove the "x" part of our string and convert the rest to a number. And for the "c = 0" part of our string, remove the " = 0" part of the string and convert the rest.

Here's how that would look like in code:

INPUT

```
def root_finder(quadratic):
    split_result = quadratic.split(" + ")
    print(split_result)
    a = int(split_result[0].replace('x^2', ''))
    b = int(split_result[1].replace('x', ''))
```

```
c = int(split_result[2].replace(' = 0', ''))
print(f"a = {a}, b = {b}, c = {c}")
sqrt_part = ((b)**2 - (4*a*c))**(1/2)
pos_root = (-(b) + sqrt_part)/(2*a)
neg_root = (-(b) - sqrt_part)/(2*a)
print(f"Positive root = {pos_root}. Negative root =
{neg_root}")
```

OUTPUT

What gives? Why is there no output? Well, what we have defined here is a function. We have not actually called that function. To fix that, insert the line root_finder("1x^2 + -8x + 12 = 0") at the bottom of your cell, and you should see the following being output:

INPUT

```
def root_finder(quadratic):
  split_result = quadratic.split(" + ")
  print(split_result)
  a = int(split_result[0].replace('x^2', ''))
  b = int(split_result[1].replace('x', ''))
  c = int(split_result[2].replace(' = 0', ''))
  print(f"a = {a}, b = {b}, c = {c}")
  sqrt_part = ((b)**2 - (4*a*c))**(1/2)
  pos_root = (-(b) + sqrt_part)/(2*a)
  neg_root = (-(b) - sqrt_part)/(2*a)
  print(f"Positive root = {pos_root}. Negative root =
  {neg_root}")

root_finder("1x^2 + -8x + 12 = 0")
```

OUTPUT

```
['1x^2', '-8x', '12 = 0']
a = 1, b = -8, c = 12
Positive root = 6.0. Negative root = 2.0
```

Okay, we see our final output at the end. Now let's dive into our function definition line by line so we can see what is happening:

```
def root_finder(quadratic):
```

This line states that we are naming a function called root_finder. It accepts a value (a.k.a. an argument) which we will assign to the variable named quadratic.

```
split_result = quadratic.split(" + ")
print(split_result)
```

These two lines will split our input string into something called a list based on the locations of the substring +. A list is simply a container for multiple other values. We can then access those values individually to read them or even write over them. The .split(" + ") syntax is a little bit weird. But basically, all strings in Python (which quadratic is going to be) have a method associated with them called split. It basically acts as a scissor that will cut up a string into parts based on the string (the delimiter) you put in. To call the split method, we use the . operator since it is part of the methods associated with a general type of variable. There are other methods such as replace associated with the string operator as well (we'll see that later on).

After that, we assign the value from our split call to the variable split_result and then we print split_result. The output of that first print call gets us the first line of output ['1x^2', '-8x', '12 = 0']. That means that our split call gave us a list of three elements '1x^2', '-8x', and '12 = 0'. Note, the ' represents that the value is a string (i.e., a mix of text, numbers, and other characters).

Next, we have the following:

```
a = int(split_result[0].replace('x^2', ''))
b = int(split_result[1].replace('x', ''))
c = int(split_result[2].replace(' = 0', ''))
```

Let's start off with the first line. We will take the first element of the list `split_result` (well, in Python, the first element of a list is actually the "zero-th" element of the list), and we will replace the string x^2 with an empty string. We will then call the `int` function on whatever is produced from that function call. So what does all of this allow us to do? Let's run it (mentally) on our first value in the split_result array. `split_result[0]` gets us `'1x^2'`. Doing `'1x^2'.replace('x^2', '')` gets us `'1'`. We can't do mathematical operations on a piece of text. Rather we need to get the number from that text. We are specifically trying to get out an integer (whole number) from the text, so we call `int(split_result[0].replace('x^2', ''))` or equivalently in our example `int('1')`, to get a = 1 at the end.

For the other two, we follow a similar pattern: * `int(split_result[1].replace('x', ''))` means we go from `int('-8x'.replace('x',''))` to `int('-8')` to -8. * `int(split_result[2].replace(' = 0', ''))` means we go from `int('12 = 0'.replace(' = 0',''))` to `int('12')` to 12.

Now, a, b, and c are all the numbers we want. But to make sure, we call the following function:

```
print(f"a = {a}, b = {b}, c = {c}")
```

Looking at the associated output, a = 1, b = -8, c = 12, we can see that it isn't quite what we expected (why aren't we printing out the braces?). It turns out that adding the f in front of the string you input into the `print` function gives the print function some special properties. It will actually *interpolate* (i.e., include) the value of variables (wrapped in curly braces) within the string passed to `print` as an argument. As a result, we get the values of a, b, and c in our output.

The rest of our function is relatively the same until the following:

```
sqrt_part = ((b)**2 - (4*a*c))**(1/2)
pos_root = (-(b) + sqrt_part)/(2*a)
neg_root = (-(b) - sqrt_part)/(2*a)
print(f"Positive root = {pos_root}. Negative root = {neg_root}")
```

Here, I assign the values of the positive root function and the negative root function to the variables pos_root and neg_root. I also print out these values at the end (using the string interpolation concept I mentioned before).

And the last line is just a call to our function with the argument "1x^2 + -8x + 12 = 0" where the " indicates that the argument is a string:

```
root_finder("1x^2 + -8x + 12 = 0")
```

> **Side Note**: Since our function is self-contained, we do not need to call it within the same notebook cell. We can actually call this function from a new notebook cell. The only thing to keep in mind is that we need to rerun the notebook cell containing the function definition if we change that function itself. This will write over the previous function stored in the notebook's memory. If you don't rerun the cell, you would be running the old version of the function (which has led to programming snafus in the past). To be safe, just rerun any cells that contain function definitions.

Minor Improvements: If Statements

Congratulations, you have written your own quadratic solver. But there are a few things we should be mindful of. First, we need to make sure that our input is in the right format. By "right format," I mean that it should contain at least two " + " substrings and end with " = 0". It should also contain "x^2" and "x". Believe it or not, we can test for these things in our function.

INPUT

```
def root_finder(quadratic):
  if (quadratic.find("x^2 ") > -1 and quadratic.find("x ") > -1 and
      quadratic.find(" = 0") > -1):
    split_result = quadratic.split(" + ")
    if (len(split_result) == 3):
      print(split_result)
      a = int(split_result[0].replace('x^2', ''))
      b = int(split_result[1].replace('x', ''))
      c = int(split_result[2].replace(' = 0', ''))
      print(f"a = {a}, b = {b}, c = {c}")
      sqrt_part = ((b)**2 - (4*a*c))**(1/2)
      pos_root = (-(b) + sqrt_part)/(2*a)
      neg_root = (-(b) - sqrt_part)/(2*a)
      print(f"Positive root = {pos_root}. Negative root =
      {neg_root}")
    else:
      print("Malformed input. Expected two ' + ' in string.")
  else:
    print("Malformed input. Expected x^2, x, and = 0 in string.")

root_finder("1x^2 + -8x + 12 = 0") # Expect to get out 6.0 and
2.0
print("SEPARATOR")
root_finder("1x^2 -8x + 12 = 0") # Expect Malformed input.
```

OUTPUT

```
['1x^2', '-8x', '12 = 0']
a = 1, b = -8, c = 12
Positive root = 6.0. Negative root = 2.0
SEPARATOR
Malformed input. Expected two ' + ' in string.
```

The major changes to our function are the addition of `if` statements. If statements allow us to generally do the following:

```
if (this statement is true):
    execute this code
else:
    do something else
```

In our case, our first if statement is the following:

```
if (quadratic.find("x^2 ") > -1 and quadratic.find("x ")
> -1 and
    quadratic.find(" = 0") > -1):
```

There are a couple of things to cover here. First, `.find` is another method associated with strings in Python. It will try to find for the string passed in as an argument and return the *index* of that string (i.e., the starting location of the string you're looking for in the string it is called on, starting numbering as 0). If it doesn't find the string you're looking for in the string you're calling .find on, it will return -1. Effectively, this means that we will be looking for the strings x^2, x, and = 0 in our input (quadratic).

> **Side Note**: If I didn't include the space after "x" in the second find call, the function would technically execute, but it wouldn't produce the expected behavior. Why? Let's look at the input: "1x^2 + -8x + 12 = 0". If I ask Python to look for "x," it will return 1 because the first time x shows up is at the first indexed position (second letter in human terms, recall that Python starts numbering at 0). Clearly, we want it to be something the ninth index (tenth character). We can fix that by including the extra space to the argument since the only time we see an "x" followed by a " " is after -8.

56

Now we need to deal with the ands in that line. and is a logic operator that is basically asking whether the statements to the left and to the right are true or not. For a well-formed input, we would expect that the find statements `quadratic.find("x^2 ") > -1`, `quadratic.find("x ") > -1`, and `quadratic.find(" = 0") > -1` are all greater than -1 (i.e., exist in our string) and satisfy the inequalities (e.g., x^2 exists at index 1 which is > -1, so `quadratic.find("x^2 ") > -1` is True). If all of the previous examples are true, then the code block under the `if` (indented one "level" beyond the `if`) is executed. If not, Python will look for a keyword `else` or `elif` (a.k.a. else if: only used if you want to check another condition before going to the else) at the same level of the `if` statement. To check if something is at the same level as another statement, just visually see if they are vertically aligned with each other or not. If they are, they're at the same level.

If the input does not have x^2, x, or = 0, then we execute the else that prints out `"Malformed input. Expected x^2, x, and = 0 in string."`

We also see another if statement further on:

```
if (len(split_result) == 3):
```

This actually helps check to see if we see two " + " substrings within our input format. Why does it do that? Recall that `split_result` will produce a list that cuts of a string when it sees " + ". In our prior example, we showed that split_result will make a list that has three elements. That means that if we have a well-formed input, we would expect to see a list that has three elements as well. We can check to see if that is true by passing in `len(split_result) == 3` to our `if` statement. `len` is a function that will find the length of whatever is passed to it (usually a list or a string). The `==` is the equality logical operator. It determines if the left side is equal to the right side.

57

> **Side Note**: Other common equality operators you'll
> see are < (meaning left is less than right), <= (left
> is less than or equal to right), > (left is greater than
> right), >= (left is greater than or equal to right), ==
> (left is equal to right), != (left is not equal to right),
> and in (left is contained within right, only to be used
> when right is something called a "dict" or a list).

Since our normal input will produce a split_result list of length 3,
we expect the equality check to pass in this case. If not, we go to the else
at the same level as this if and find that it will print out "Malformed input.
Expected two ' + ' in string.".

Last change:

```
root_finder("1x^2 + -8x + 12 = 0") # Expect to get out 6.0
and 2.0
print("SEPARATOR")
root_finder("1x^2 -8x + 12 = 0") # Expect Malformed input.
```

Here, we call root_finder twice. The first time we expect to get
outputs 6 and 2. We then print the word "SEPARATOR" (just to help
visually separate outputs), and then we call root_finder on a malformed
input that does not have the correct format (we need to see a " + " after the
x^2). In our output, we see that the if statement for that failed and see the
following overall as expected:

```
Positive root = 6.0. Negative root = 2.0
SEPARATOR
Malformed input. Expected two ' + ' in string.
```

More Improvements: File Input and For Loops/Iteration

Let's say we want the user to also be able to supply a .csv file (.csv or CSV = comma separated values file, a format similar to an excel sheet) containing a single column with the header "Formula," then read the .csv, and then call our function.

First, let's make a csv with some example formulas:

Formula
1x^2 + -8x + 12 = 0
2x^2 + -9x + 12 = 0
3x^2 + -8x + 8 = 0
4x^2 + -7x + 12 = 0
5x^2 + -10x + 12 = 0

Save this csv file as "input.csv" file (can be done in Excel. Note: make sure that you select the type to be a CSV file).

In Colab, go to the side bar, and click the folder icon. Click the upload icon and then upload the "input.csv" file. You should see the following in your file menu (refer to Figure 3-2).

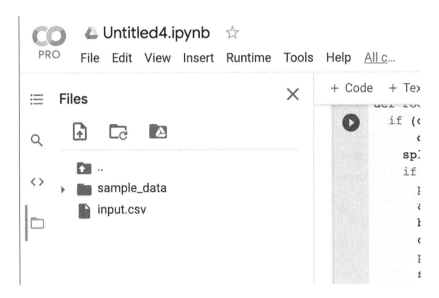

Figure 3-2. *This is the location of the file upload menu in the Colab side pane. Upload your input.csv file here*

Now, we need to somehow process an input .csv file.

We can do that by editing our code to the following:

```
import csv

def root_finder(quadratic):
  # ...same as before

def read_file(filename):
  with open(filename) as csv_file:
    csv_data = csv.reader(csv_file)
    for idx, row in enumerate(csv_file):
      if (idx > 0):
        root_finder(row)

read_file("input.csv")
```

If we execute that, we should see the following output:

```
['1x^2', '-8x', '12 = 0\n']
a = 1, b = -8, c = 12
Positive root = 6.0. Negative root = 2.0
['1x^2', '-9x', '12 = 0\n']
a = 1, b = -9, c = 12
Positive root = 7.372281323269014. Negative root =
1.6277186767309857
['1x^2', '-8x', '8 = 0\n']
a = 1, b = -8, c = 8
Positive root = 6.82842712474619. Negative root =
1.1715728752538097
['1x^2', '-7x', '12 = 0\n']
a = 1, b = -7, c = 12
Positive root = 4.0. Negative root = 3.0
['1x^2', '-10x', '12 = 0']
a = 1, b = -10, c = 12
Positive root = 8.60555127546399. Negative root =
1.3944487245360109
```

It seems like those are the expected outputs. But let's take a deeper look at what we've just done.

In the first line of the block, we have a line that says import csv. This line allows us to use some functionality that Python does not load by default but is nonetheless included in the Python standard library (collection of tools that are useful to have without installing anything else). The csv library allows us to read and write csv files without worrying about the complexities associated with validating its format and making the system calls to do so.

Next, we move on to the new function read_file. Read file takes an argument filename which (as we see in the last line) will be a string of the name of our csv file.

Note   If we were to put this file in a subfolder, we would need to specify this argument as `"SUBFOLDERNAME/CSVNAME.csv"`.

Next, we have the line

```
with open(filename) as csv_file:
    csv_data = csv.reader(csv_file)
```

This statement actually opens our csv file and the `with` keyword will key Python into making sure that we delete its location in memory once we are done using it (otherwise, it would stick around forever, or at least until we shut down this notebook). We then ask the `csv` library to read the csv file. It produces a CSV `Reader` object (think of this as a set of functions and variables packed into a single word) that is assigned to the variable `csv_data`.

> **Side Note**: Objects are pervasive throughout programming. They are a construct that allow programmers to easily call and execute functions and get properties that are interrelated to each other. To get an understanding of what objects are, we have to understand how they are made. Objects are made via other things called "Classes." These classes specify the properties and methods that make up an object. Here is an example class that holds a name, age, height, and weight for a patient and also calculates a BMI for that patient:

```
# Define the class Patient which has properties age, height,
and weight
class Patient:
  def __init__(self, name, age, height, weight):
```

```
        self.name = name
        self.age = age
        self.height = height
        self.weight = weight
    def get_bmi(self):
        return self.weight / ((self.height)**2)
```

```
# Instantiate a patient object with specific age height and
weight
bob = Patient("bob", 24, 1.76, 63.5)
# print out bob's BMI
print(bob.get_bmi()) # outputs: 20.499741735537192
print(f"Bob's height is {bob.height}m. His weight is {bob.
weight}kg.")
# The above outputs: "Bob's height is 1.76m. His weight is
63.5kg."
```

We define a class (called Patient in this case) that has properties name, age, height, and weight. The method called __init__ is in charge of processing the values we use to instantiate (i.e., create) an object using the class. Here, all we do is tell Python to keep track of the arguments we supply. We do this by assigning properties to self. Breaking down this statement further, when we write self.name = name, we are telling Python "create a *property* called 'name' and set it equal to the argument name" that I passed into this function). We do this for all the other properties as well (but we could do fancy things like validate our input values). We also create a method on the object called get_bmi. By default, all methods that intend to access values associated

with a class must have one argument called `self`.
We can then use the properties from that object in
the method body itself. Here, we make a `get_bmi`
method that will return a BMI for a patient (based
on taking their weight, which can be accessed via
self.weight, and dividing it by its height squared).
When we run `bob = Patient("bob", 24, 1.76,`
`63.5)`, we create an instance of the `Patient` class
(a.k.a., we have made a Patient object) and have
assigned it to the variable bob. We can call the
`get_bmi` method on the bob instance we made just
by typing a `.` followed by the name of the method.
We can also get at any other properties on the `self`
object by running `variable_of_the_instance.`
`name_of_the_property`. In this case, if we want to
access bob's height, we write `bob.height` as we do
in our string interpolation statement of this code
sample. There are many other things we can do with
objects, but this is just the beginning.

Next, we have the following:

```
for idx, row in enumerate(csv_file):
  if (idx > 0):
    root_finder(row)
```

Now what does this `for` statement do? Think about the structure of
our csv file. There is a header which will be present on the first row (or
the zeroth row in Python's counting system). Then each of the rows that
follow will contain each of the quadratics we want to evaluate. If we knew
how to get our csv file to be equivalent to a list (like we saw earlier), we
could just individually enumerate which indices of that list we want to
run root_finder on. For example, let's say that the rows in our csv were all

in a list called quads. quads[0] would give us our csv header ("Formula" in this case). quads[1] would give us 1x^2 + -8x + 12 = 0, quads[2] would give us 2x^2 + -9x + 12 = 0, and so on. We could call our root finder function just by passing each of these into the method as follows: root_finder(quads[1]). However, this is inefficient as we don't know ahead of time how many rows are in our csv file. Instead we can use a for loop. This allows us to say "for each item in a list (or some other collection of objects that can be iterated through), do the following." In the example just mentioned, we could write something like

```
for quad in quads:
    root_finder(quad)
```

This statement allows us to assign each item in our list to the temporary variable quad. As we sequentially go through the elements in quads (i.e., *iterate* through the list), we assign each variable temporarily to quad and then pass use it in the body of the for loop (here we pass quad as an argument to root_finder). We can also get access to what element number we are on the list by wrapping our list of items in an enumerate call and rewriting our for loop as follows:

```
for index, quad in enumerate(quads):
    if index > 0:
        root_finder(quad)
```

Recall that the first element of quads would be just the word "Formula" which isn't a valid input to root_finder. So we only run root_finder if the index is > 0 (i.e., we aren't running it on the first a.k.a. zeroth element which is equal to "Formula").

We are basically doing the exact same thing with enumerate in our original code. Except in this case, we can actually call enumerate on the csv_file variable containing the reader object. We can do this because the reader object has specific implementation properties that make it "iterable" (i.e., a for loop can be used on it). By extension, we can wrap it in an enumerate call and temporarily assign the index value we are at in the loop sequence to idx and the value of that row to row. We then only call our root_finder function when the idx is > 0.

The last line of interest just contains read_file("input.csv") which calls our read_file function with the input.csv filename.

File Output, Dictionaries, List Operations

Currently, we output the results from our root_finder call to standard output (i.e., the console). It would be nice if we could output it to a csv file that has one column called "equation," containing the original equation, "positive root," and another called "negative root" to contain the results. Each row would correspond to the original equation.

Let's see how that would be written out:

```
import csv

def root_finder(quadratic):
  if (quadratic.find("x^2 ") > -1 and quadratic.find("x ") > -1
  and
      quadratic.find(" = 0") > -1):
    split_result = quadratic.split(" + ")
    if (len(split_result) == 3):
      a = int(split_result[0].replace('x^2', ''))
      b = int(split_result[1].replace('x', ''))
      c = int(split_result[2].replace(' = 0', ''))
      sqrt_part = ((b)**2 - (4*a*c))**(1/2)
      pos_root = (-(b) + sqrt_part)/(2*a)
      neg_root = (-(b) - sqrt_part)/(2*a)
      return (pos_root, neg_root)
```

```python
    else:
      print("Malformed input. Expected two ' + ' in string.")
      return None
  else:
    print("Malformed input. Expected x^2, x, and = 0 in string.")
    return None

def read_write_file(input_filename, output_filename):
  answers = []
  with open(input_filename) as csv_file:
    csv_data = csv.reader(csv_file)
    for idx, row in enumerate(csv_file):
      if (idx > 0):
        answer = root_finder(row)
        if answer != None:
          positive_root, negative_root = answer
          answer_dict = {
              "equation": row,
              "positive root": positive_root,
              "negative root": negative_root,
          }
          answers.append(answers_dict)
  if len(answers) > 0:
    with open(output_filename, 'w') as csv_output_file:
      fieldnames = ["equation", "positive root", "negative
      root"]
      csv_writer = csv.DictWriter(csv_output_file,
      fieldnames=fieldnames)
      csv_writer.writeheader()
      for a in answers:
        csv_writer.writerow(a)

read_write_file("input.csv", "output.csv")
```

This is complicated, but let's break down what the changes are:

1. In `root_finder`, we have now removed some print
    statements (kept the ones that print in cases of input
    errors). And we added `return` statements. Return
    statements allow us to pass values between functions
    and assign the output of functions to variables. `print`
    statements that we have been using until now do not
    enable us to capture the output and assign that to
    a variable. Here, we return either the `pos_root` and
    `neg_root` in the form of a tuple (data structure that
    contains two values) or the value None which is a
    reserved word in Python that doesn't equal anything
    except another value/variable equal to None. We do
    this so we can check whether the output is valid or
    not (if it isn't, the output will be equal to None).

2. We have renamed `read_file` to `read_write_file`
    since it now contains another function (writing a
    file). The arguments have changed; we now accept
    two arguments, the input filename and the output
    filename.

Let's dive deeper into the body of the `read_write_file` function. In
order to write results to a csv file, we have to keep track of the results that
we have accumulated so far. We will use a list to do so.

> **Side Note**: Lists are a common structure used
> to hold data (a.k.a. a data structure) in Python.
> As the name would imply, they typically are just
> a list of individual objects, variables, or other
> values. Lists can be assigned to other variables
> (just as anything else in Python), and we can
> access individual elements of a list by writing
> `list_variable[index]` where `list_variable` is the

variable equal to your list and index is the number
of the element you want to access. Note that lists
always start their numbering at 0, so if you want
to get the first element of the list, you would write
list_variable[0]. What if you wanted to get the
last element of a list? Well, you would somehow
need to know the length of the list itself. That can
be accessed by wrapping your list_variable in
a len() call like so len(list_variable). To get
the last element of the list, we would do list_
variable[len(list_variable)-1] (we must
use the -1 at the end since we start numbering at
0). A shorthand for the earlier example is just to
do list_variable[-1]. In the case that you try
and access a list element that does not exist (e.g.,
list_variable[len(list_variable)]), you may
get an error that says something along the lines of an
IndexError saying that the list index is out of
range. That usually means that you tried to access
an element that doesn't exist and you should go
back to your code and make sure you're counting
from 0. We can make a new list just by typing in
list_variable = ['element 1', 'element 2'],
but what if we want to add more elements to this
list after we initially create it? Well, all we need to
do is call list_variable.append(something). This
will add a new element (equivalent to something)
to the end of our list. We can find elements in a list
by doing list_variable.find(value_of_element_
you_want_to_find). Lastly, you can remove an
element from a list by doing list_variable.
remove(value of element to remove).

Each element of the list will have to somehow contain the original equation, the positive root, and the negative root. These values can be packed together in a single construct called `Dictionary`. A dictionary allows us to specify a set of "keys" and "values" in a single contained statement. A "key" is a reference name we use to look up an associated "value." For example, we could make a dict as follows:

```
bob = {
    "name": "Bob Jones",
    "height": 1.76,
    "weight": 67.0
}
```

And then access properties by writing the `variable name['key name we want']`. Note: in the following code sample, I write what is outputted as a comment (i.e., words following the # symbol):

```
print(bob['name']) # Bob Jones
print(bob['height']) # 1.76
print(bob['weight']) # 67.0
```

We can also edit the dict as follows:

```
bob['gender'] = 'Male' # adds a key "gender" and set it equal
to "Male"
bob['height'] = 1.75 # edits the current value of height from
1.76 to 1.75
print(bob) # {'name': 'Bob Jones', 'height': 1.75, 'weight':
67.0, 'gender': 'Male'}
```

In this case, we want to somehow write to an output csv file each of our results from the `root_finder` function. The columns we will output, a positive root, a negative root, and the original equation, correspond to the keys we would use in to make a dictionary with the respective values being derived from the results from the `root_finder` function (for the positive/negative root) or the original input itself (the equation). Hence, in our read_write_file method, we have the following (read the comments above each code line to understand the flow of the program):

```python
def read_write_file(input_filename, output_filename):
  # Initialize an empty list called "answers" which we will put
  results into
  answers = []
  # ...then open the csv file
  with open(input_filename) as csv_file:
    # ...then create a CSV reader object to read the CSV row by
    row
    csv_data = csv.reader(csv_file)
    # ...then iterate through the csv file by row
    for idx, row in enumerate(csv_file):
      # ...after the header row (in the header row idx = 0, we
      don't want
      # to input that in the root_finder function, so we only
      look for
      # rows after the header where idx > 0).
      if (idx > 0):
        # ...get the result of `root_finder` called on that
        equation
        answer = root_finder(row)
        # ...if the input was valid (and we have an answer)
        if answer != None:
          # ...then get the positive and negative root of that
          answer
          positive_root, negative_root = answer
          # ...then create a dictionary with keys equal to the
          columns we
          # will report
```

```
        answer_dict = {
            "equation": row,
            "positive root": positive_root,
            "negative root": negative_root,
        }
        # ...and lastly append that dictionary to the answers
        list
        answers.append(answers_dict)
    print(answers) # this is new, but allows us to see what's in
    the answers list
```

Note, the last line of the previous code snippet is new, but if you run the function with that new line entered, you should get an output similar to the following:

```
[
{'equation': '1x^2 + -8x + 12 = 0\n', 'positive root': 6.0,
'negative root': 2.0},
{'equation': '1x^2 + -9x + 12 = 0\n', 'positive root':
7.372281323269014, 'negative root': 1.6277186767309857},
{'equation': '1x^2 + -8x + 8 = 0\n', 'positive root':
6.82842712474619, 'negative root': 1.1715728752538097},
{'equation': '1x^2 + -7x + 12 = 0\n', 'positive root': 4.0,
'negative root': 3.0},
{'equation': '1x^2 + -10x + 12 = 0', 'positive root':
8.60555127546399, 'negative root': 1.3944487245360109}
]
```

It will likely appear on a single line for you, but regardless, you should see five pairs of opening and closing braces ({}) indicating that we have a list of five elements. One additional thing to note: in this output, we see the characters \n. This is a special set of character used to note a line break (i.e., that someone pressed "enter" on their keyboard and that the next thing should be printed out on a separate line). Since we are printing an array, Python ignores making a new line for these \n characters, but in any normal situation (e.g., if you were printing a regular string such as print("Hello\nWorld")), you would see the letters before the \n on one line and the letters after \n on the other line. There are also other characters preceded by \ that can denote other special printing behaviors (e.g., \t denotes a tab).

Next, we move on to actually writing that list to a file. It turns out that Python has a handy way of writing a list of dictionaries to a csv file so long as all of the dictionaries have the same set of keys. We do satisfy that condition since all of our dictionaries have an equation, positive root, and negative root key.

```python
# if the answers list is not empty (i.e. we have at least one
result)
if len(answers) > 0:
  # write to the output file we specify
  with open(output_filename, 'w') as csv_output_file:
    # set fieldnames (these will be the columns) equal to the
    keys of
    # our dictionary.
    fieldnames = ["equation", "positive root", "negative
    root"]
    # initialize a CSV writer object
    csv_writer = csv.DictWriter(csv_output_file,
    fieldnames=fieldnames)
    # write the column headers
    csv_writer.writeheader()
    # for each answer (temporarily referred to as 'a') in the
    answers list
    for a in answers:
      # write a new csv row
      csv_writer.writerow(a)
```

This code snippet looks relatively familiar to reading a csv. The only things different are that in our open statement, we must specify that we are writing to a CSV file by passing in a second argument `'w'`. Additionally, since we are writing a CSV file, we also need to specify the field names (a.k.a. columns) we will be writing in our csv and also write the column names first (which we do with `csv_writer.writeheader()`).

Cutting This Down with Pandas

A bit of bad news. What we just spent section doing can be done in about six lines of code:

INPUT

```python
import pandas as pd

def read_write_file_with_pandas(input_filename,
output_filename):
  df = pd.read_csv(input_filename)
  results = df['Formula'].apply(root_finder)
  results = results.dropna()
  if (len(results) > 0):
    df[['positive root', 'negative root']] = results.tolist()
    df.to_csv(output_filename)
    display(df)
  else:
    print("No valid results")

read_write_file_with_pandas('input.csv', 'output.csv')
```

OUTPUT

```
Formula                positive root   negative root
1x^2 + -8x + 12 = 0    6.000000        2.000000
1x^2 + -9x + 12 = 0    7.372281        1.627719
```

```
1x^2 + -8x + 8 = 0      6.828427        1.171573
1x^2 + -7x + 12 = 0     4.000000        3.000000
1x^2 + -10x + 12 = 0    8.605551        1.394449
```

We can drastically cut down on the code we have to write by importing libraries outside of Python's standard library system. One of those libraries is called "pandas," and it is very good at manipulating datasets of information (especially csv data) and outputting results.

In the first line, we will import the pandas library and assign all of its functionality to the variable pd as follows:

```
import pandas as pd
```

Next, we will define another read and write function that takes in the same arguments as our previous read_and_write_file function.

Then we will use pandas read_csv function to read in our CSV files containing our input formulas. We can access the read_csv function using pd.read_csv (note, we prepend library-specific methods with the name of the library or the variable we assign to that library, in this case pd). We pass in the name of the file we want to read to pd.read_csv and store the result in a variable called df.

pd.read_csv produces a data structure known as a data frame. It is basically an excel sheet in Python's memory, and if you were to write print(df) or display(df) in the body of the function, you would see that the variable contains a table with a single column named Formula just as our CSV input sheet contains.

Next, we will run our root_finder function on each of our rows by calling df['Formula'].apply(root_finder). df['Formula'] gets us the column named "Formula" (which is our only column) in the data frame. The .apply method on the df['Formula'] column is then going to call the function passed to its single argument on each of the rows of the df['Formula'] column. In this case, we called .apply(root_finder), meaning that we run root_finder on each of the rows in the formula column. We then store those values to the results variable.

Recall that our `root_finder` function outputs a tuple (data structure containing two values) containing the positive and negative roots or the value None. We will first remove any None values by calling `results.dropna()`. This will remove (a.k.a. "drop") any invalid numbers. We assign the result of that call back to the variable `results` so we can continue to manipulate that variable (but we could have made a new variable name).

If the length of the `results` variable is greater than 0 (i.e., we have valid results), we will then actually unpack the values in each tuple into corresponding columns `positive root` and `negative root`. Pandas, by default, has no easy way of separating a tuple into distinct columns. Instead, we must convert the `results` variable we have to a `list` (using `.tolist()`) and then assign the resulting lists to column names. Pandas will automatically understand that a list with multiple elements in it should be separated into multiple columns. All we need to do is specify the names of those columns like so.

```
# We create two columns 'positive root' and 'negative root'
that
# are equal to the result from `results.tolist()`
df[['positive root', 'negative root']] = results.tolist()
```

Lastly, we write the CSV file to the filename we specified as the output csv filename using `df.to_csv(output_filename)`. And we then display the data frame we have worked with so far to the user using `display(df)`.

The point of showing the earlier example was to get you introduced to the idea that libraries are potentially useful for helping cut down the code you need to write. The authors of the pandas library have already put in a lot of thought into how to read and manipulate data from CSV files and have probably put in more error checking than we can feasibly do in this chapter. Thus, it is advisable to use a library when you can so long as you understand what the library is roughly doing behind the scenes.

Side Note: When we imported pandas into our Python script, we did so using `import pandas as pd`. We didn't have to install pandas on our system. However, this is only the case in the Colab environment we are working in. Usually, you will have to install a library yourself if you are developing in Python directly on your computer (rather than through a cloud interface as we are doing now). In that case, you will need to use a *package manager* such as `pip` to help you install the libraries you need to work with. If we were to install pandas on our local system, we would write in our terminal: `pip install pandas`, and that's it!

Summary

In this chapter, we went through an example where we created a program to solve a quadratic formula and even handle file input. We saw how we can use variables, for loops, if statements, file input and output, dictionaries, objects, and lists to help make this task easier. These programming language constructs within Python took us all the way from hard coding in the individual values to use in our quadratic equation solver to allowing Python to handle all the heavy lifting of actually manipulating the numbers.

As we go forward in this book, each of these individual concepts will become vital to your understanding and usage of machine learning algorithms. File input/output will help you load in large datasets into Python. Dictionaries, objects, and lists will help you store and manipulate all of that information in logically arranged pieces. For loops and variables will be used all the time to store information and iteratively process your dataset.

In the next chapter, we will cover machine learning concepts from a "bird's eye view." There won't be much programming in the following chapter, but there will definitely be more after that.

## CHAPTER 4

A Brief Tour of Machine Learning Algorithms

Now that we've covered the basics of how to program and some of the data structures in Python, let's switch our focus back to the theoretical and conceptual concepts of machine learning (ML) that were touched upon in the first chapter. This time around, we'll start talking about specifics for each of these algorithms, namely, focusing on what their inputs and outputs are and how they work (at a high level; going any lower than that involves a fair amount of math that isn't worth discussing in an introductory book).

ML Algorithm Fundamentals

ML algorithms typically go through a process of "training" followed by an evaluation period called "testing." The training process for most algorithms roughly follows this rough pattern: (1) Make algorithm see a subset of data. (2) Make an initial guess for the thing we want to predict from that data (e.g., predict what type of cancer is present in an image, predict whether individual is at risk for diabetes). (3) See how wrong that guess was (if we

© Abhinav Suri 2022
A. Suri, *Practical AI for Healthcare Professionals*,
https://doi.org/10.1007/978-1-4842-7780-5_4

have "ground-truth" data). (4) Adjust internal structure for how predictions are made, hopefully in a direction that leads to less error. (5) Repeat (usually until there is no marked improvement in results on the dataset we've exposed the algorithm to).

The training process itself can run multiple times as the ML algorithm will run over a subset of the data you feed it called "training data." Once the algorithm is appropriately trained, it is evaluated on a set of data (called "testing data") that was never exposed to the ML algorithm in the training process. Why do we care about making sure that the algorithm never saw the data before? Well, we want to make sure that the algorithm actually is learning something about the structure of the data rather than just memorizing individual data points (i.e., "overfitting"). By testing on a holdout set that wasn't used to train the data, we can evaluate the algorithm and get a sense as to how it would perform in the real world.

> **Side Note**: During the training step of the ML algorithm, we may also want to test out different configurations of the ML algorithm we choose or even compare multiple ML algorithms. One approach to do so would be to train on some subset of our data and then evaluate using the remainder of the data. However, this leads to inadvertent overfitting of the testing data since you would be tuning your ML algorithm parameters to perform well on the test set. Ultimately, we should be absolutely blind to the test set until we are ready to evaluate its performance in the last step of development.
>
> So if we shouldn't evaluate on the test set while trying out different parameters/ML models, how can we compare performance? Well, we can just split up our training set into a training set and validation

set. In that case, we would just use the validation set to evaluate our trained network across multiple ML configurations/models, pick out the best one, and then test that out on the testing set as the final step. Often, you'll see something along the lines of a 60% train, 20% validation, and 20% test split of the underlying data. This means that 60% of the data was used to train the ML algorithms, 20% was used to validate/compare configuration/multiple ML models, and the last 20% of the data was used to test the ML algorithm selected after validation. You can split your data in other ways as well (e.g., 80% train, 10% validate, 10% test), but you should ensure that you have enough test data to get an accurate sense of how your algorithm performs in "real-world" conditions (e.g., only testing on two or three data points wouldn't be that useful since the probability of something working out by pure chance alone is relatively high).

ML algorithms generally break up into two major categories (there is technically a third category, but we'll skip over that in this book): "supervised learning" algorithms and "unsupervised learning" algorithms.

Supervised learning algorithms require that we have "labels" on our data. By a "label," I mean that the data has some outcome that is either a classification or continuous measure (e.g., heart disease status, predicted survival probability). Our data usually has multiple characteristics (predictors) associated with the final label itself. Accordingly, when we evaluate how well these supervised algorithms do, we compare what the ML algorithm outputs as the label for a given datum point to the actual label for that point. We can then report the accuracy, sensitivity, specificity, ROC, etc., of these algorithms once evaluated on the test set.

Unsupervised learning algorithms are run on data that does not have labels. Instead, they try to optimize another metric. For example, an unsupervised clustering algorithm may focus on trying to find clusters of data that are closely related to each other. The result to optimize in this case is how closely related the data points are to each other (e.g., the distance between data points) within a cluster vs. between clusters (we would want data to be closely related to each other within a cluster and different from data in other clusters). The algorithm in this case would be trying to optimize how data points are assigned to clusters. Here, we don't need any information about the data itself other than the characteristics that describe a data point (i.e., we don't need anything along the lines of a final diagnosis, etc.). The outputs from unsupervised learning tasks can be very helpful in exploratory data analysis. For example, in genetics studies, an unsupervised learning algorithm can be used to differentiate samples based on gene expression levels. The resulting separation between samples could yield insights into difference between the samples which yield areas for further investigation.

The following is a set of summaries on individual algorithms in the space of machine learning. Note: this list isn't meant to be exhaustive by any means. Rather it is meant to give a rough understanding of the different types of ML algorithms that exist and how they work. Very minimal math will be used in these explanations except where absolutely necessary (so this won't be very rigorous).

Regression

This class of ML algorithms deals with trying to go from data points to continuous (i.e., numerical) values. Probably the first regression algorithm people learn is linear regression which focuses on finding a "line of best fit" that goes through the data points on a two-dimensional scatter plot with an X and Y direction. However, note that any of these regression techniques can work with multidimensional data. In terms of ML, we don't try to visualize these multidimensional data since our data can often be "wide" (i.e., have multiple predictors per datum point). Rather, we will focus on trying to find the best line (for two-dimensional data), plane (for three-dimensional data), or hyperplane (for N-dimensional data where N is any number) to fit our data points. We'll start off our exploration of regression techniques with linear regression. From there, we'll move on to logistic regression which can help predict probability of an outcome (between 0 and 1). Lastly, we'll talk about LASSO and Elastic Net for Regression (these algorithms help ensure that we don't include too many variables in our models). Note, I mention the word "model" several times which is defined as follows: a model is just an instance of an ML algorithm that can be trained or evaluated.

Linear Regression (for Classification Tasks)

Linear regression comes in many different flavors. Perhaps the most useful is ordinary least squares (or least squares linear regression). This algorithm operates off of the principle of trying to minimize "the sum of squared residuals" (SSR). What's that? Well, it is a measure of how "bad" our proposed linear regression equation is. Let's take a simple example.

Imagine we have patients who have been given a weight loss drug and we want to find out how many pounds they lose while on the drug during a certain time period. The outcome we would like to predict in this case is pounds lost, and the input would be characteristics of the patient, such as their starting weight, age, diabetes status, BMI, and how many minutes of exercise they get in any given week.

After the linear regression algorithm is run, the algorithm gives us a predicted value for the amount of weight a patient would lose. This should try to represent the trend while also minimizing how "wrong" it is for individual data points. To do this, the algorithm is set up to minimize a "residual," that is, how far off was the algorithm's prediction for weight los compared to the actual weight loss for that patient. It will then square that residual since some of the predicted values will be below the actual value and some will be above (we square those residuals to ensure that values don't cancel each other out). Formally, for each patient p, we find

$$\text{residual} = \left(\text{predicted weight lost for p} - \text{actual weight lost for p}\right)^2$$

Then it sums up all of those residual values to come up with a value called the sum of squared residuals. This is the quantity that ordinary least square regression attempts to minimize. Some calculus actually shows there is a "closed form" solution to linear regression using this method (i.e., it can run in one step). Accordingly, the algorithm finds the appropriate slopes and intercepts. At this point, the model is finished training, and we have a general equation that can predict how much weight someone loses after being on a weight loss drug. We need to then determine how well the algorithm works on real-world data (in our held out test set).

The output from this algorithm is very interpretable. In most Python libraries (and even in Excel), you can get a list of the slopes for each of the variables that contribute to the regression along with an intercept, resulting in an equation that looks generally like

$$\text{weight lost} = \text{intercept} + \beta_1\left(\text{starting weight}\right) + \beta_2\left(\text{diabetes}\right)$$
$$+ \beta_3\left(\text{BMI}\right) + \beta_4\left(\text{exercise}\right)$$

where β_n represents a slope. If we tried to actually graph the results of this linear regression onto a graph, we may be out of luck since there are five dimensions (four predictor dimensions + one output dimension), and it is hard to depict anything above a three-dimensional graph on a computer. Rather we can take a look at the absolute values for the β_n (betas) and see which ones are the largest. From there, we can make a reasonable assumption that the betas that are the largest contribute most to the outcome. In a variety of epidemiological studies, linear regression is widely used especially when trying to quantify the effectiveness of an outcome (e.g., effect of a healthiness campaign on weight loss) given some individual data.

Logistic Regression

Logistic regression is similar to linear regression in that it can take in multiple possible predictors and find slopes/intercepts that would make a line, slope, or hyperplane of best fit. However, the primary distinction between linear regression and logistic regression is the range of output values that come from these functions. Linear regression outputs values that can range from negative infinity to positive infinity. However, logistic regression can only output values from 0 to 1. Given the restricted output range of logistic regression, it lends itself very well to applications involving prediction of likelihoods/probabilities and can help predict a binary outcome (e.g., disease vs. no disease) since a disease state could be encoded as 1 and a no disease state can be encoded as 0. In medical applications, logistic regression models are typically applied to case-control studies since the betas can be interpreted as odds ratios (see side note) once exponentiated, yielding a large degree of interpretability.

The logistic regression equation we attempt to fit is as follows:

$$y = \frac{e^{\beta_0 + \beta_1 * X + \beta_2 * X \dots}}{1 + e^{\beta_0 + \beta_1 * X + \beta_2 * X \dots}}$$

Simplifying further

$$\ln\left(y / (1-y)\right) = \beta_0 + \beta_1 * X + \beta_2 * X \dots$$

The left-hand side of this equation is equivalent to what we would normally consider to be the natural log of the "odds" of something (i.e., the probability of something happening, y, divided by the probability of something not happening, 1-y). Accordingly, we can plug in values for X (our predictors for an individual) and find the odds of them having the event y. However, in most cases (such as a case-control study), we will not be able to report the odds alone (since a case-control study has preset sizes of the disease, i.e., "case" population, and the normal, i.e., "control" population). Rather, we can take the ratio between two predicted odds of separate individuals and determine an odds ratio.

For example, if we were predicting the probability of developing lung cancer given someone's prior smoking history, we could fit a logistic regression equation on individuals in a case-control study. We would only have two betas in this case, the intercept (β_0) and β_1 (for indication of prior smoking history). Let's say that β_0 equals 1 and $\beta_1 = 3.27$. If we wanted to compare the odds of developing lung cancer for a smoker vs. a nonsmoker, we would calculate $\dfrac{e^{1+3.27*1}}{e^{1+3.27*0}} = 26.31$. We can say that an individual who has a history of smoking has 26.31 times the odds of developing lung cancer compared to an individual who has no smoking history. Note, I substitute $X = 1$ in the case that someone has a smoking history and $X = 0$ if they do not (X acts as an indicator variable here).

> **Side Note**: Output values from the logistic
> regression equation can also be thought of as
> predicting probabilities (i.e., a value ranging from
> 0 to 1 indicating the how likely something is to
> happen where 1 = will happen, 0 = will not happen).
> While logistic regression outputs these values on
> a continuous scale, we can institute a "threshold"
> value that would turn the continuous prediction
> into a binary outcome (less than threshold or more
> than threshold). This can be useful in tasks such
> as predicting disease outcomes. However, the
> value of the threshold is something left up to the

programmer. One easy threshold to pick may be 0.5; however, another threshold such as 0.7 may work better (may help us eliminate any "false positive" predictions at the expense of making some false negative predictions). False positive (FP) predictions indicate that the output predicted that the patient was a positive case when they really weren't (these lead to higher healthcare expenditures and unnecessary treatment). On the other hand, false negatives are when the prediction is that the patient does not have an outcome of interest but really does (these lead to misdiagnoses, which can be detrimental if the condition is critical). We also care about true positives and true negatives which occur when the machine prediction matches up with the true status of the patient (i.e., they are actually a case or actually not a case, respectively). We can use the true positive, true negative, false positive, and false negative to generate false positive rates/sensitivities and specificities.

To see how our logistic regression model performs in multiple scenarios, we can generate something called an "ROC curve." The ROC (receiver-operator characteristic) curve comes from finding the true positive rate and false positive rate at multiple thresholds. We then plot these data points (x = false positive rate or sensitivity, y = true positive rate or 1-specificity) on a graph and connect the points to generate a curve that looks like the following (refer to Figure 4-1 for ROC curve, refer to the following for definitions for sensitivity and specificity)

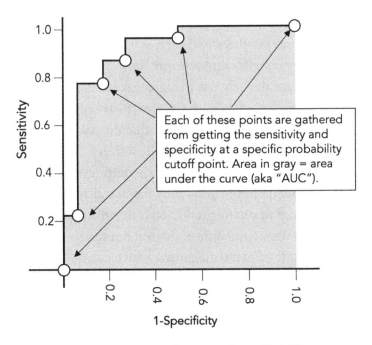

Figure 4-1. Received operative characteristic (ROC) curve example

where points A, B, and C are sensitive/1-specificity
pairs generated from different threshold values.
We can then calculate an area under the curve
(AUC) that can give us a better idea how to compare
different classifiers (AUC values range from 0 to
1 where 1 = perfect predictor and 0 = worse than
random, higher AUC is generally better).

Sensitivity a.k.a. "recall" can be calculated from the
following formula:

$$\text{Sensitivity} = \frac{\# \text{of true positives}}{\# \text{of positives} + \text{false negatives}}$$

Specificity can be calculated as follows:

$$\text{Specificity} = \frac{\#\,\text{of true negatives}}{\#\,\text{of true negatives} + \#\,\text{of false positives}}$$

) Medical researchers often separately report sensitivity and specificity (in addition to the ROC curve) at the threshold that produced the highest sensitivity and specificity in the ROC curve.

In order to actually fit a logistic regression equation, we can use a method called maximum likelihood estimation (MLE) to do that for us. MLE operates in a similar fashion to ordinary least squares regression (i.e., it tries to minimize some function that relies on minimizing how "wrong" it is); however, it does not have a closed form solution. Rather it must attempt to find the optimal set of betas that will fit the equation by trying out multiple betas, seeing which ones minimize how "wrong" it is and then adjusting those betas accordingly to further minimize the error.

Logistic regression is probably the most useful and interpretable form of regression used in the healthcare space. While it is not considered to be a buzzword in the machine learning space, it is a tried and tested method for handling predictions involving probability of a certain outcome.

LASSO, Ridge, and Elastic Net for Regression, the Bias-Variance Trade-Off

Sometimes we come across the situation where we have so many predictors in our dataset that it may benefit us to try and cut down or minimize the number of predictors we have. The primary benefit of doing so is to aid in the interpretability of the final model itself by distilling down 100s of independent variables to something more manageable such as a few dozen. We can do so through two methods, LASSO or Ridge Regression (Elastic Net is a combination of the two).

Before we get to these algorithms, we need to discuss the bias-variance trade-off in machine learning. When we train a model, we can prioritize trying to make sure that our best-fit line touches all the data points in our training data. While this would minimize all the error in our training dataset, we could see huge differences in performance on our test dataset since testing data may not necessarily be equivalent to our training data. In this situation, we say that a model has high variance since its results vary quite a bit depending on the data used to evaluate its performance. We can also say that this model would have low "bias" which means that the line of best fit makes no assumptions about the underlying structure of the data since it just tries to fit everything given all of the parameters available to it. Alternatively, we could make another line of best fit that just tries to go straight through the points (but not touching all of them). This model would be considered to have high bias since it makes assumptions about the underlying structure of the data (namely, that it is linear); however, it may have low variance since the linear line of best fit does a decent job of fitting both the test set and the training set.

At both extremes, we have a high degree of error in our dataset. When variance is high and bias is low, we have a large degree of error since our test set does not fit to our model (i.e., we have overfit the training data). When bias is high and variance is low, we also have a high degree of error since the model may be too simple/makes too many assumptions (i.e., we have underfit the training data). Our goal is to try and find a "sweet spot" that helps us minimize our overall error in these situations. One way to do that is through regularization methods which selectively remove variables from our model (i.e., help minimize variance and while slightly increasing bias) and find a happy medium in the trade-off. LASSO, Ridge Regression, and Elastic Net are all regularization algorithms.

LASSO works by adding a term to the sum of squared residuals equation we talked about earlier. In addition to calculating the error between predicted and actual values for given data points, LASSO adds a term that is equal to the sum of the absolute value of our betas times a

parameter called "lambda" we set ourselves (this parameter is called a
hyperparameter since we set it rather than letting the computer set it).
This extra term is called the "L1 norm." Thinking about what this means,
we can see that if we have a large number of beta terms, we're increasing
the new sum of squared residuals formula. Since the goal is always to
minimize the sum of squared residuals (SSR), the algorithm selectively
sets betas equal to 0. Doing so minimizes the additionally added LASSO
term. We can also tune how "important" getting rid of betas is in LASSO
by setting lambda equal to a high value (i.e., more important to get rid of
betas) or a low value (i.e., less important to do so). We can also try out a
bunch of different lambdas on our validation set within the training set.

Ridge Regression operates similar to LASSO regression except that it
adds the sum of the betas squared times lambda to the regular SSR formula.
This extra term is called the "L2 norm." Ridge Regression differs from
LASSO however since Ridge Regression does not completely set certain
betas to 0 (i.e., it does not completely get rid of them). Rather it keeps all of
the features and just reduces the betas for the unimportant ones.

Elastic regression is a compromise of the two. It adds the L1 norm and
the L2 norm to the SSR equation with a separate hyperparameter called
"alpha" determining which norm is weighted heavily (as alpha increases,
L1 norm/LASSO is more important; as alpha decreases, L2 norm/Ridge is
more important). As a result, we get a happy medium between LASSO and
Ridge Regression and help prevent ourselves from overfitting our data.

In prior studies, Elastic Net has proven to be incredibly useful in
helping remove variables from cohort studies that use data containing over
1000 characteristics per data point (i.e., very "wide" data given that there
are many columns/characteristics associated with a single row of data).
As a result, we can get a measure of variable importance in the ultimate
model that is fit (since unimportant variables are either eliminated or are
minimized to near-zero values). To find the optimal value of alpha and
lambda for these studies, these studies often undertake a procedure called
a "grid search" which means they try out every possible combination of

alpha and lambda values (each limited to a certain range) on the training data and then see which produces the best results on the validation set. The model trained with alpha-lambda parameter combination that gives the best results will then be evaluated on the test set.

> In the real-world usage: In 2015, Eichstaedt et al. published their model on how Twitter could predict county-level heart disease mortality. In this paper, they basically downloaded data from Twitter, cleaned the data, and extracted common words and phrases. They used those words and phrases as independent variables in a regression model, where the dependent variable was the rate of atherosclerotic heart disease incidence in the county the tweet came from. Since this problem was boiled down to a simple regression, they were able to leverage the regularization algorithms we talked about, specifically Ridge Regression. Applying that algorithm allowed them to also extract "variable importance" which, in this case, were the words that most influenced the disease incidence rate in the regression formula. They ultimately found that counties where tweets contain angry/depressing words/tones have higher rates of heart disease. Importantly, this predictor, when combined with county demographic statistics, was an incredibly accurate predictor of heart disease incidence.

While we've been talking about regression, the simple relationship between variables and the outcome may not be something that can be modeled with a simple equation. Rather, we may need to know something about the actual points of data that have gone into training a model to find out what the classification is of a new point. That's why we're going to take a look at instance learning algorithms which allow us to capture relationships directly based on prior data points.

Instance Learning

Instance learning algorithms try to perform classification or regression by comparing an unknown data point's output directly to values used to train the network. In regression, we saw how we would first try to fit an equation (either a linear equation or logistic equation) and then predict values from these equations. Outside of helping finding the optimal equation, the underlying points of data aren't actually used in regression techniques. Instance learning algorithms use the individual training data points to determine the class or value of the test point. We'll explore two ways this task can be done: k-nearest neighbors and support vector machines (SVMs).

k-Nearest Neighbors (and Scaling in ML)

K-nearest neighbors is an algorithm that is nonparametric (i.e., it doesn't make assumptions about the form of the output function). Compared to regression techniques (which make assumptions about the ultimate form of the equation), nonparametric methods are much better at handling data that does not have a clear x-y relationship. The issue with these methods is that you cannot find ways to reduce the number of parameters needed to find valid predictions.

K-nearest neighbors algorithm works as follows: (1) For a given test point, find the k closest points to that test point (where k = a number of points that you specify). These are the k-nearest neighbors. (2) In the case of classification tasks, the predicted class of the test point will be the majority of the classes of the k-nearest neighbors (e.g., if the four nearest neighbors were "diabetic," "diabetic," "diabetic," and "non-diabetic," the test point's class would be diabetic). In the case of a regression task (here, "regression" just means to output a continuous value rather than distinct classes), we simply take the average values of the k-nearest neighbors (e.g., if the four nearest neighbors to a test point had values of 50, 60, 70, and 80 kg, the output value for a test point would be (50+60+70+80)/4 = 65 kg).

There are some additional considerations to take into account: what value of "k" do we use and what type of metric for distance do we use.

An optimal "k" can be determined by trying out all possible values of k in your training-validation set. Once you find a "k" that minimizes your objective for error (e.g., accuracy in the class of classification), you can then evaluate your function. For distances, we can use Euclidean distances (similar to finding the hypotenuse of a triangle), Manhattan distances (similar to getting a "real-world" distance between points on a city grid), and much more. Some of these distances may be suited better for certain tasks (e.g., Manhattan distances are preferred when handling data that is high dimensional), but you should try out several distances to see which one produces optimal results.

Another important note is that the K-nearest neighbors algorithm is highly susceptible to changes in scaling. For example, if one dimension of your data measures someone's height (usually constrained between one and two meters) and another dimension measures their weight (in the 10s to 100s of kg), we might have difficulties finding the closest points in each dimension since their scales are so different from each other. We could also be susceptible to the effects of outliers in our data as well. To help solve this issue, we can instead center and scale our data. Doing so basically means to reassign the values of our dimensions to a z-score (i.e., the original value - mean of values in that dimension/standard deviation of values in that dimension). In that case, most values will be between -2 and 2 (if normally distributed) regardless of the scale.

To aid in interpretability, we can also try and output what the decision boundaries are for classification in k-nearest neighbors at various levels of "k" (as is done in Figure 4-2).

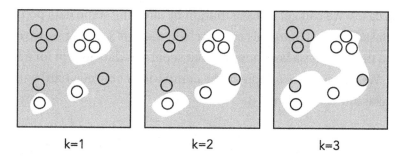

Figure 4-2. *K-nearest neighbors example. Here, we can see how modifying k can lead to different decision boundaries between the white and gray classes of points*

Here, each pixel in the graph is colored the class of the k-nearest neighbors output given a specific k. When k is small, we can see that the boundaries between white and gray areas of the graph are highly irregular which makes sense since fewer points are used to classify an object. When k is large, we see that the decision boundaries are more regularly shaped due to the fact that it takes a larger number of k-nearest neighbors for a class to be in the majority. The larger k values may provide a better understanding of how points are actually separated from each other, but may also misclassify some points. However, when k is small, we may be learning decision boundaries that are not that useful and that may only work on the training data.

Support Vector Machines

I'll only mention this algorithm in brief since it tends to get very math laden when diving into the details. The support vector machine algorithm operates on the assumption that there may be a line, plane, or hyperplane that separates two classes of data. The goal is to find that separation so that the margin between the ultimate plane and the actual data points is the highest it can possibly be (i.e., find the line that can perfectly separate two classes of data, a.k.a. a "hard margin"). However, in some cases, we can get a larger margin by allowing some data points to be misclassified (this margin is called a "soft margin"). Doing so, we can get a line that still has a large margin that separates data except for a few outliers. We can see an example of the comparison between hard and soft margin classifiers in Figure 4-3.

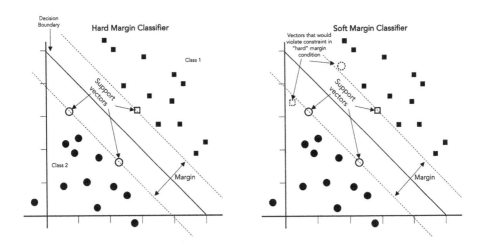

Figure 4-3. *SVM margins for both hard and soft margin classifiers. "Support vectors" are denoted as hollow circles or squares. Circles or squares that violate the hard margin assumption are marked with dashed borders. The decision boundary is a solid black line with margins that are dashed*

Here, the image on the left represents a hard margin classifier since none of the circles or squares points cross the "margin" boundaries around the line. The image on the right represents a soft margin classifier since some of the circles/squares are allowed in the margin region around the line even if they violate the previous margin.

Occasionally, we will have to perform transformations on our data (such as squaring it) to find an optimal line, plane, or hyperplane that separates data points from each other. There are a number of possible transformations that we can apply to our data, and support vector machines help us find the optimal transformation to apply that gives us a plane that best separates the data at hand. For example, in the following case (Figure 4-4), we can use the SVM algorithm to find the plane that best separates this data.

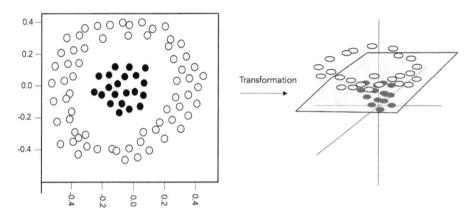

Figure 4-4. *SVM used on an example that would be difficult to linearly separate in two dimensions*

On the left-hand side, it would be difficult to find a line or polynomial that can separate the classes of this data appropriately (where the color of the point represents its class). However, if we apply a transformation to the data (in this case, a transformation called the radial basis function kernel), we can find a plane that separates this data for us. The SVM algorithm gives us the ability to find this plane. SVM can be implemented to work for regression tasks as well.

> In the real-world usage: Son et al. published the usage of support vector machines in 2010 for predicting whether heart failure patients would adhere to their medication. Their input data points had predictors of gender, daily frequency of medication consumption, medication knowledge, New York Heart Association functional class,

ejection fraction, Mini-Mental Status Examination score, and whether or not they had a spouse. Their output was whether the heart failure patient was taking their medication or not. They were able to achieve a detection accuracy of close to 80% which is impressive given that they had a small dataset of 76 individuals. SVMs have since been used in a number of medical prediction applications, including the prediction of dementia, whether or not a patient needs to be admitted, and more. Similarly, k-nearest neighbors has been used to determine whether individuals are at risk of developing heart disease based on previous data on patients.

Decision Trees and Tree-Based Ensemble Algorithms

Decision trees help produce some of the most interpretable results in the ML world. Decision trees are not quite like actual trees. Rather, they're structured like an inverted tree with a root on top and leaves and branches that increase in number as you go further down, as seen in Figure 4-5.

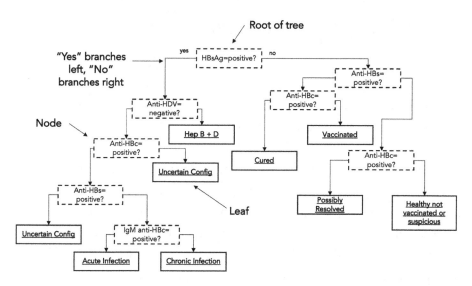

Figure 4-5. *Structure of a decision tree for predicting Hep B and D infection/recovery/unknown status*

At the top, there is a root (formally called a node) and that has a left and right branch. Each branch also has a node (which also has its own left and right branches and so on). Some of these branches do not split further into other left/right branches (these are called leafs). In decision tree making algorithms, a decision rule will be learned for each node of a tree. That node would be something along the lines of "If the patient has a positive Hep B surface antigen titer test, go to the left branch; otherwise, go to the right branch." These branches have their own decision nodes as well until they get to the point that there is a leaf node which usually gives a classification for the patient (e.g., they have a disease vs. they don't have a disease) or gives some number which represents the average labeled value of other instances of your training data that reached that part of the decision tree.

The key parts of the decision trees that need to be learned are what characteristics to "split" on (i.e., test at each node) and whether it would be worth splitting on that characteristic or not.

Classification and Regression Trees

Classification and regression trees (CART) is a machine learning algorithm that allow us to learn a decision tree. The algorithm works by iteratively trying out characteristics to split on. Whichever split yields the best result is the one chosen to apply to the data (making a new node in the tree with branches based on that rule). The algorithm then tries to find new splits for each of the branches. However, this algorithm is not necessarily the best since it only relies on picking the best split at that point in time rather than trying out multiple different trees to see what works the best once the entire algorithm is run. This type of algorithm is known as a "greedy" algorithm (in this case, the algorithm is greedy since it decides the split that's best once seen at a single point in the training process).

But how do we evaluate which split is the "best"? For classification tasks, we can use a term called "Gini impurity." Gini impurity can be calculated at each node by multiplying the proportion of training points at that node in one class by its complement (1 – the proportion). We sum these values across all of the classes and weigh values at each node to determine which splitting characteristic would lead to the lowest possible Gini impurity coefficient (0 = all instances allocated to each branch are of the same class which means we have a perfect classifier; anything higher means that there are instances that are misclassified at each node). In an equation, the Gini impurity coefficient can be expressed as follows:

$$G = \sum_{i=1}^{C} p(i) * \left(1 - p(i)\right)$$

where G is the Gini impurity coefficient, C represents the classes to split on, and $p(i)$ represents the proportion of points in the given class i.

However, if we were to just find the best possible tree, we could get a very complex tree with hundreds of nodes and branches if we don't penalize its growth. After all, we're trying to find a tree that is interpretable. We can institute a "stopping criterion" which places a restriction on tree growth if there aren't enough elements generated by splitting at a particular branch (e.g., if a split pushes one data point to the left and three to the right, but our stopping condition stipulates that we must have, at minimum, five elements at a node, we won't split on that criterion). We can also "prune" the tree by setting a hyperparameter called "Cp" (short for complexity). This adds a term to the Gini impurity score that penalizes the number of smaller trees (subtrees) created under a particular node (higher number of subtrees penalizes the growth of trees more). Both of these measures help ensure that we do not engage with creating trees that are too complex and can't be used in practical decision making.

You should also be aware that there are multiple versions of decision tree algorithms. CART relies on the Gini impurity score to find the best tree; others such as ID3, C4.5, and C5.0 rely on another measure called "information gain." It isn't important to understand the exact details of how it works, but it is useful to know that there are other decision tree algorithms to try out on your dataset.

Tree-Based Ensemble Methods: Bagging, Random Forest, and XGBoost

Ensemble methods in the decision tree world help optimize predictions by creating multiple trees and allowing each tree to give a "vote" on a particular outcome. The simplest of these algorithms is called bootstrapped aggregation (a.k.a. "bagging"). Bagging involves creating multiple trees similar to the CART algorithm; however, it bootstraps the training dataset, meaning that it randomly selects subsets of the training set to create trees. It samples with replacement, meaning that a training sample can appear multiple times. However, since the trees are all trained on subsets of the training data, it can be more robust to the data in general since it would be less prone to overfitting. In the evaluation phase, all of these trees give a "vote" on what the correct classification should be based on the branches and nodes for each tree. The majority prediction wins.

Random forest is another machine learning algorithm that builds on bagging. Instead of just selecting samples of the training set with replacement and building multiple trees, random forest also selects random subsets of characteristics to split on for each node in each tree. For example, if each patient in your dataset has 100 characteristics you keep track of, random forests will create many trees that will only use some subset of the 100 characteristics to split on at each node (e.g., 20, 30, 42,...). The number of randomly selected characteristics can be changed through a hyperparameter known as "k" or "mtry." Usually, mtry is set to be 1/3 of the total number of characteristics (33 in our example case), but you should try out a number of values for mtry. You can also set the number of trees to be generated in random forests (usually using more trees is better; however, returns diminish after a high value of trees that you'll need to fine-tune). Some machine learning libraries also give you the opportunity to specify how "deep" these trees can be (this basically limits the amount of times a tree can branch) since trees that are too deep (and have many branches) can overfit the training data.

XGBoost is another ensemble algorithm that produces a similar output to random forests; however, it builds these trees through a method known as gradient boosting. Random forest builds its "forest" of trees independently from each other, while gradient boosting builds one tree after another, adjusting the influence each tree has on the ultimate decision. It does so by adjusting a weight assigned to each tree based on a "learning rate" hyperparameter (basically determines how much the weight can change in one training iteration). If the learning rate is too high, we may never find the optimal solution or may stumble into a somewhat optimal solution that only works on our training data. If the learning rate is too low, we may take forever to find the optimal solution. Most libraries out there will suggest values to use for your XGBoost algorithm or automatically provide them to you. XGBoost-generated trees can be much better than random forests; however, they often take a while to train compared to random forests.

In the real-world usage: Chang et al. showed in 2019 that C4.5 decision trees and XGBoost were used to predict clinical outcomes among patients with hypertension. The predictors they use are physical examination indicators (sex, age, BMI, pulse rate, left arm systolic pressure, thyroid function [FT3], respiratory sleep test O2, systolic blood pressure [at examination and at night], and number of hypertensive drugs), and the output is whether the patient had a myocardial infarction, stroke, or other life-threatening events. They ultimately find that XGBoost achieves the best accuracy (94.36%) and AUC (0.927) compared to normal decision tree-based algorithms (C4.5 trees achieved an accuracy of 86.30%). This paper highlights how ensemble algorithms can provide a significant advantage over tree algorithms.

Clustering/Dimensionality Reduction

Algorithms in this class are typically considered to be unsupervised learning algorithms. Accordingly, there's no real measure of accuracy or error that we can refer to using these algorithms; however, we can still get a general sense of how well they performed. Unsupervised algorithms are incredibly useful for clustering and dimensionality reduction.

Clustering algorithms generally operate to find which points of data are closely related to each other, forming a "cluster." This can be useful for determining the locations of outbreaks and also determining how many groups of patients there are that share common characteristics in a large dataset.

Dimensionality reduction does exactly what its name implies. These algorithms help us reduce the number of different factors we're considering to aid in the plotting and interpretation of high-dimensional data. These algorithms are often used in population genetic studies where individuals have 1000 "dimensions" (i.e., genetic locations of interest) and need to be somehow separated to explain differences in subgroups.

k-Means Clustering

k-Means clustering works by trying to find clusters of data points that are closely related to each other. At a high level, the algorithm first randomly selects "k" number of data points to be the centers of each cluster. Other data points are then assigned to one of the "k" clusters based on which cluster it is closest to it. Once points are then assigned to a cluster, the center of the cluster must then be updated to account for all the new points that have been added (this center may not overlap with an existing point). This process of assigning points to clusters and updating the center position continues until the algorithm reaches "convergence" (i.e., the centers do not continue to change significantly, and the points assigned to specific clusters do not continue to change). This process is illustrated in Figure 4-6.

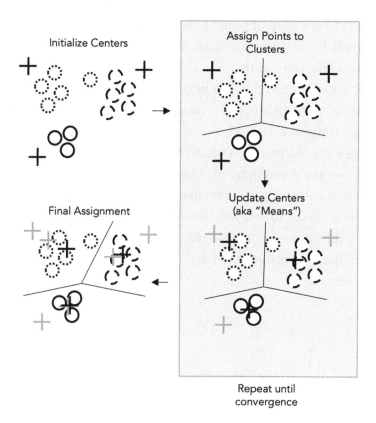

Repeat until
convergence

Figure 4-6. *k-Means algorithm steps. Black crosses indicate the centers at that step. Light gray crosses indicate centers from previous steps (note how the crosses across the steps). Note, the steps enclosed within the gray rectangle are repetitively done until the centers reach convergence*

k-Means obviously has one major hyperparameter which you must tune: the number of clusters (i.e., the number of centers) you want to find in the dataset, k. Sometimes, if you have prior knowledge about the dataset, you may know what "k" you want (e.g., if you know that there are diabetic and nondiabetic people in the dataset a good k is 2). Other times, you don't know an optimal "k" and just want to find the best possible clustering for your data (at which point you could explore characteristics of the points in each cluster to get a sense as to how the clusters are differentiated from each other).

Finding a best k without prior knowledge can be done using the elbow method. It operates on the idea that we should try and find clusters that are closely packed together, a.k.a. the within cluster sum of squared errors (WSS). We can find the WSS by determining the distance of each point to the center of the cluster it is assigned to; we want to find the k for which we get the lowest WSS. However, after some number of k, the WSS typically does not decrease by a significant amount. At one extreme, we could set k to equal the number of points we have in our dataset; however, that may not be valuable since a small k could give us the opportunity to get a diverse cluster to analyze. We define the point at which there are diminishing returns as the "elbow" which can be identified by plotting the WSS against the k value that generated the WSS. An example of an elbow plot can be seen in Figure 4-7.

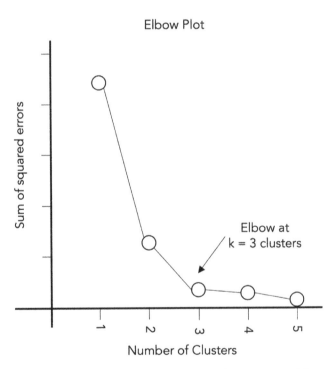

Figure 4-7. *Elbow plot example with an elbow around k = 3*

Here, we can see around k = 3 clusters there is an "elbow" in the graph (i.e., a sharp decrease in the WSS lost upon adding an additional cluster, a.k.a. diminishing return). There are also other methods such as the silhouette method that takes into account how similar a point is to its own cluster vs. how similar it is to other clusters (in this method, a silhouette score is produced for each k attempted, and the highest silhouette score is considered the optimal number of clusters). Another measure called the gap statistic can also help identify the optimal number of clusters by calculating the within cluster variation with the expected values determined from a null reference distribution (generated from bootstrapping). The k that produces the highest value gap statistic is the one with the optimal number of clusters.

Variations on the k-means clustering algorithm can also produce a hierarchical cluster where we produce a dendrogram (a tree where closely related points are closer to each other on the tree; see Figure 4-8).

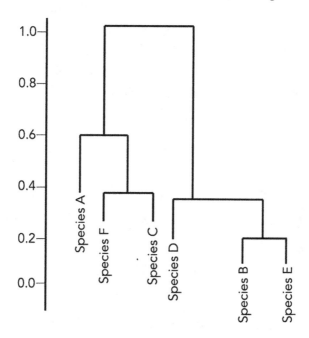

Figure 4-8. *Example of a dendrogram that depicts relatedness between species*

These trees are often used to measure evolutionary relationships between species or can even model the relationships between microbiota in our gut (based on the similarity of DNA between species found in microbiota samples).

It is important to note that k-means clustering is sensitive to scale, meaning that we need to rescale and center our data when using these methods (similar to k-nearest neighbors).

Principal Component Analysis

Principal components analysis (PCA) can help us visualize high-dimensional data. It does so by identifying combinations of predictors that can make new axes. We can then use these new axes to replot our data in a manner that helps show the degree of variation in the data itself. The final end product of PCA is a set of axes (called principal components) which are combinations of multiple dimensions. We can use some of these axes (usually the first two) to plot out our existing data but in a new coordinate system. In some cases, this can help data that does not appear to be differentiated to appear much more different/separable compared to just visualizing them on a single pair of axes. An example of a PCA transformation can be seen in Figure 4-9.

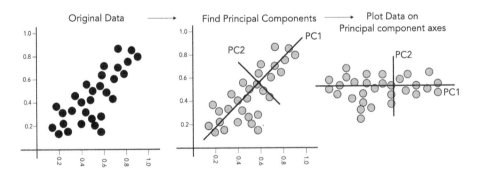

Figure 4-9. *PCA transformation steps. First, data is plotted, then PCA axes are found, and then data is transformed to PCA space where data is replotted on the new axes*

Roughly, PCA aims to find principal component axes that maximize the variance in data when projected onto that axis. To see what that means, refer to Figure 4-10.

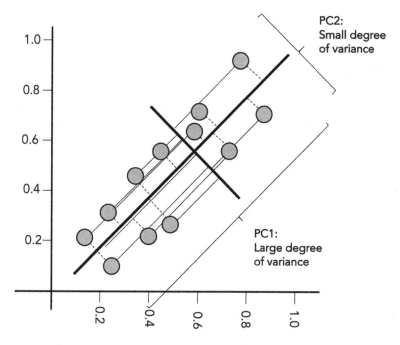

Figure 4-10. *Variance along PC1 and PC2 is depicted here. Note how PC1 has a higher variance compared to PC2*

In this image, we can see that the black lines would make good axes since they would allow us to see the differences between points clearly. These axes are combinations of whatever characteristic is described by the x axis and a little bit of the characteristic described by the y axis. We then continue to find other axes that can help separate the points from each other once the prior axis is applied to the data. Eventually, we get a ranking of the principal components (of which there are many) followed by the % of variation they can explain. We choose to use as many principal component axes that can explain a large degree of variation until there is a point of diminishing returns (this can be assessed via a "scree plot" which looks similar to the plots generated by the elbow method in k-means clustering).

Artificial Neural Networks and Deep Learning

Artificial neural networks (ANNs) and deep learning (DL) are considered to be the darling of the ML world at the moment. These algorithms help extract information from input data to generate an "intermediate" representation of the input data. That intermediate representation will usually be some transformation of the input which can be used to easily "learn" which aspects of that transformed input are best predictors of the output. We saw how transforming the input played a role in getting SVMs to work so well for classifying data, but these transformations take SVM to a whole other level, routinely learning transformations that aren't usually comprehensible to humans.

When we talk about neural networks, the obvious word that pops up is "neural" indicating some relationship to a neuron. Nearly every introductory text shows how the neural network was partially inspired by a human neuron and its behavior; however, that comparison is starting to diverge greatly from where neural networks stand today. Regardless, we will cover that comparison since it is helpful for motivating the basic structure of a simple neural network.

Fundamentals (Perceptron, Multilayer Perceptron)

Neural networks are made up of individual units called neurons. Each neuron can have multiple inputs and has an output which can be fed as input into other neurons (just as biological neurons have dendrites and axon terminals that act as multiple inputs and multiple outputs, respectively; refer to Figure 4-11).

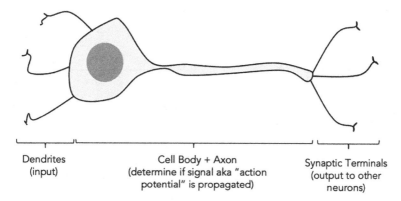

Dendrites
(input)

Cell Body + Axon
(determine if signal aka "action
potential" is propagated)

Synaptic Terminals
(output to other
neurons)

Figure 4-11. *The structure of a biological neuron*

In order for biological neurons to fire an action potential, the membrane potential needs to surpass a specific threshold. Similarly, artificial neural networks can be engineered to mimic that behavior (though that may not be true in all neural networks).

Moving away from the biological thinking behind an artificial neural network, the actual implementation of ANNs involves two primary constructs: weights and biases. For each input to an artificial neural network, a weight multiplies the input by some number. The bias is a number (either positive or negative) that is added to the sum of all the weighted inputs. Usually some function (a.k.a. an "activation function") is applied to that final sum of the weighted inputs and bias: sometimes that function is simply the identity (i.e., the sum itself), sometimes it a sigmoid function (constrains the final value between 0 and 1), and sometimes it could be another function that is equal to the final sum of weights and biases only if that sum is positive; otherwise, it is zero (this is called a ReLU function). A picture of an artificial neuron can be found in Figure 4-12.

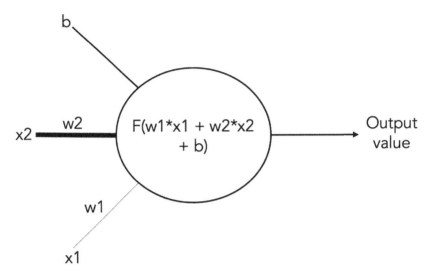

Figure 4-12. *Artificial neuron (a.k.a. "perceptron") with inputs x1 and x2 and bias term. Note that w1 and w2 can take on different values as indicated by the differences in thickness of lines*

In this image, we can see that this unit of the ANN (formally called a "perceptron") has two inputs, X1 and X2, and an output. It also has a bias noted as "b" and weights for each of the inputs called "w1" and "w2." We also see that a function "f" (the activation function) is applied to the sum of the weights multiplied by the inputs plus the bias to produce the final output.

Many perceptrons can be arranged together to form a layer of a neural network. Many of these layers can be chained together to form a type of artificial neural network called a multilayered perceptron, a.k.a. an MLP (like in Figure 4-13).

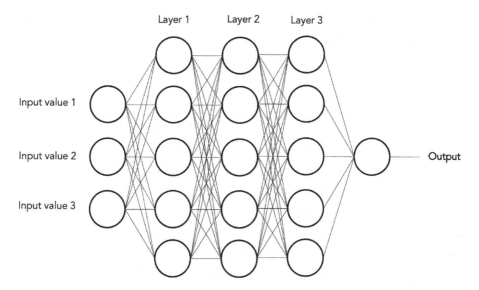

Figure 4-13. *Full multilayer perceptron with three inputs, three fully connected layers, and an output*

An MLP usually has a first layer that is considered to be the input layer. Each perceptron at this layer takes on a value of either one of the characteristics of a data point in tabular data (e.g., rows in a spreadsheet) or could even represent values for pixels in an image (one perceptron per pixel). This input layer then is densely connected (i.e., each perceptron connects to all other perceptrons in the next layer one time) to the next layer of perceptrons. These perceptrons can then be fed into another layer and so on. Finally, the second to last layer is usually fed into either a single or multiple output perceptrons. A single perceptron output would be useful if we're just trying to predict a number given some input values. Multiple perceptron outputs would be useful if we want to predict a class for the input data (e.g., no diabetes, prediabetic, diabetes). In the classification task, we would find the output perceptron that produces the highest value or can even get something akin to a probability of an input belonging to a class designated by each output perceptron (by applying a function called "softmax").

113

You may have noticed we've included quite a lot of perceptrons in this example, but what is the advantage of including so many perceptrons in our network? Consider that each neuron can take in multiple inputs and transform those inputs into an entirely different number. Each of those numbers can then feed into other neurons that output different numbers and so on. In each of the layers of the MLP, we transform the input of the network into something else entirely. Some of these representations may make it easier for these networks to find rules that work best for classification or regression tasks.

One topic we haven't touched on until now is how the network actually learns the correct weights and biases for each of these connections and perceptrons. ANNs do this through a process called "backpropagation." Essentially, a training data point (or multiple training data points, a.k.a. a "batch") is sent through the network, and a set of outputs is recorded. For each of the outputs, the network calculates how "wrong" it was per a function that we specify ourselves called the "loss function" (e.g., for regression, that error could just be how far off the output number was from the ground-truth number, squared). The goal of the network at this point is to try and find the best way to adjust each of the weights and biases present in the network to minimize the loss. The proof behind how backpropagation works can be found at multiple places online, but it does involve a fair bit of multivariable calculus. Once the network adjusts its weights and biases, it goes through new training data (or may even go through the training data again) to continue to update the weights and biases.

Importantly, you may see mentions of something called a "learning rate" which is important in determining how fast neural networks can converge to an optimal solution that minimizes its error. It does so by multiplying how much each weight and bias are adjusted after seeing some training data. In most cases, we want the learning rate to be relatively low since we do not want to overshoot an optimal solution and never reach it. However, making it too low may lead to it taking a long time for the network to converge upon a final solution. We set the learning rate itself, so it is a hyperparameter. Other techniques (such as "batch normalization" which centers/scales outputs from each perceptron in the network) can also help stabilize the learning process of a neural network.

Another major hyperparameter you may have to adjust is the number of "epochs." An epoch is a hyperparameter which defines how many times the ANN/MLP model will go through the entire dataset. There is no rule as to the amount of epochs needed to train a network, and it is entirely dependent on the network architecture. Some simpler networks may only require a dozen or so epochs to train. More complex networks could require hundreds of thousands. To help determine an optimal epoch to set, it is best to set a "stopping condition" on the training of your neural network (e.g., if the overall error a.k.a. "loss" of the network does not decrease by 10% after ten epochs, stop the training of the network). This stopping condition is important to set since neural networks can overfit the training data. To also prevent overfitting, "regularization" techniques can be used (usually involving something along the lines of "dropout" a.k.a. randomly removing perceptrons from the network or L1/L2 norm regularization that penalizes large weights, similar to what we saw in LASSO/Ridge Regression).

There are also other hyperparameters that can be set by you such as batch size (number of training data points the network sees before it can update weights), optimizer choice (there are other algorithms outside of gradient descent that determine how networks learn), weight initialization (determines the first weights and biases a network has prior to any training; usually this is random), loss function (what you're trying to optimize), layer size (how many perceptrons are in each layer of the network), and much more.

In general, MLPs are components of many popular neural network architectures in at least some part. Most complicated networks for image classification will have a final two to three layers that are just densely connected perceptrons that aid in classification or regression tasks. MLPs on their own also can be useful for predicting tabular data. However, the scale of MLPs becomes unwieldy to deal with especially when using images as input. Considering if an image is sized 400px x 400px and used as input into a network, that means that there are 160,000 input perceptrons into this network since each perceptron represents a pixel. Furthermore, each of those perceptrons will need to connect to more perceptrons in the intermediate layers of the MLP, representing even more weights and biases to learn. After a point, it becomes computationally prohibitive to use this architecture for handling images. That's where we turn to convolutional neural networks.

Convolutional Neural Networks

To help solve the issue of training neural networks to handle image inputs which are fairly large, researchers came up with the idea of applying "convolutions" to the input image itself. A convolution is just a linear operation that multiplies parts of the input images in a network and produces output values. The construct that determines how the multiplication takes place is a filter (also called a kernel). Multiplying input images by the filter will produce a smaller image. Doing this over multiple convolutions (i.e., multiple runs of the filter multiplying image input and producing an output image) can greatly reduce the size of an input and can even produce an intermediate representation (called a "feature map") of the image that the network can then learn on.

But what exactly is a filter? A filter is a set of numbers arranged into a matrix (i.e. a grid). Usually these filters are fairly small (3x3, 5x5). The numbers contained within these filters themselves are also learned by the neural network. To produce the feature map, the filter multiplies the pixel values in each 3x3, 5x5, (or whatever size the filter is) section of an input image in a sliding fashion (going left to right, then top to bottom). This multiplication operation then produces another image that may be smaller than the original input image but definitely will look much different from the input image. An example of what a convolution looks like can be found in Figure 4-14.

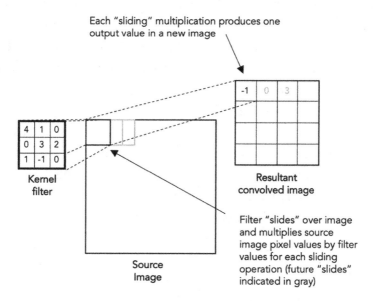

Figure 4-14. Convolutional operation on an image. Here, the filter values are multiplied across a 3x3 patch in an image. A single value is calculated by summing values from this multiplication. That value is outputted to the output image, and the filter continues to slide over the original image

In a convolutional neural network, each layer consists of a set of filters (you can specify the number) that are applied to the image input. Given that most image inputs to a neural network are color images (which have a red channel, a green channel, and a blue channel), the filters are sized to have WxHx3 elements (where W = width of the filter, H = height of the filter). There are additional parameters that describe operations of how these kernels are applied to the image. One of those parameters is called padding which helps us deal with the issue of what happens at the edges of images (if we keep moving to the right, at the right-hand size of an image, the filter will continue to move over pixels that don't exist and go beyond the image bounds). We can adjust this by adding padding to our image (usually just pixels that are valued 0) which solves this problem. We can also set the stride of the filter which dictates how many pixels the filter "skips" when moving in each direction. If we keep a stride of 1, the input and output images will have the same size. If we increase the stride, we tell the filter to move over two pixels instead of one pixel at every step, reducing the size of our input.

There are other ways to help reduce the size of input images as they pass through the network. One method is called "max pooling." This is a filter that operates by passing a filter (usually something along the size of 2x2) and stride (usually 1 or 2) and only outputs a single value (the maximum valued pixel in the patch of the image the filter is on). An example of what max pooling does to an image can be found in Figure 4-15.

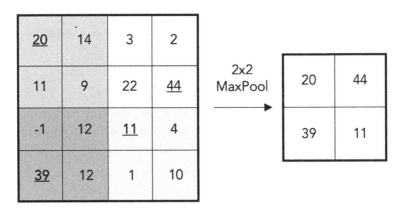

Figure 4-15. *Max pooling 2x2 operation. Note how in each 2x2 region only the maximum value is kept in the output region*

We can specify the arrangements and sets of convolutional layers we want our network to have through working with libraries that handle all of the work of setting up and managing all the filters at each step. Usually, those libraries get it down to us only needing to specify the number of filters we want at each step, the kernel size, the input image shape, the batch size (number of images used in one iteration before weights are updated), and the padding/stride. At the end of these neural networks, we will typically "flatten" the last convolutional layer by creating a layer of perceptrons that correspond to the number of pixels in the last convolutional layer output and create additional layers that are densely connected to that flattened layer. At the end, we will have a few output neurons corresponding to each of the classes we want to predict in our network.

Convolutional neural networks have been credited with ushering in the renewed interest in AI technologies. A particular convolutional network called AlexNet was able to achieve a high degree of accuracy on a standardized image classification benchmarking test called ImageNet. Google followed up with their inception network architectures and released the trained models of these networks to the public (which was especially generous given that these networks required a lot of computational power to achieve the accuracy they did). Importantly for medical imaging applications, these convolutional networks can be retrained for doing other forms of image classification. This process (known as transfer learning) typically freezes the learned filter values in the initial part of the network and only retrains the last few layers (the densely connected layers). This transfer learning paradigm allows individuals to retrain networks very quickly (even on their laptops) for new image classification or regression tasks that weren't originally trained for. Importantly, transfer learning highlights how the convolutions applied to images generate an intermediate representation that is resilient to changes in classification tasks (i.e., the network is truly learning to extract salient features from an image that can be used to learn anything).

Over the years, convolutional neural networks have had more and more layers added to them (I should mention that "deep learning" means that the networks used for a learning task have many layers/convolutional operations). This trend has resulted in the development of networks that are very large but have marginal improvements in accuracy on standardized benchmarks. There are other network architectures called "transformers" that are at the front of state-of-the-art image classification techniques that are performing better (but usually a deep convolutional network will be sufficient for most medical imaging tasks).

Other Networks (RCNNs, LSTMs/RNNs, GANs) and Tasks (Image Segmentation, Key Point Detection, Image Generation)

There are many other network architectures that exist for different tasks. Some of them may be useful for medical research; however, a fair amount of them have been limited to the technical sphere of AI and has yet to see wide adoption in the world of medicine.

Recurrent neural networks (RNNs) and long short-term memory networks are networks that can be used for dealing with data streams or otherwise time-based data. For example, the task of trying to predict likelihood of ER admission given a set of patient histories could be addressed by using an RNN or LSTM. LSTMs are considered to be more advanced than RNNs due to the fact that they solve the issue of exploring and vanishing gradients (these problems lead to the training process becoming very long or impossible). These networks have started to see their way into the world of natural language processing (i.e., interpreting text) for medical research applications.

RCNNs (or region-based convolutional neural networks) are used for the task of object detection in medical imaging. These networks can be used for the process of actually finding instances of objects within images (such as lung nodules, fractures, etc.). They also can be used for automating medical segmentation tasks (i.e., outlining various structures/pathologies) and even for landmark detection (i.e., finding relevant anatomical key points for each detected object such as the corner points of vertebral bodies for use in scoliosis detection).

GANs are used to generate images (or other data) based on pairs of images it has seen before. This network consists of two parts: a generator which is responsible for generating image proposals given some input and a discriminator which is responsible for trying to find the errors in how those new images were generated. The generator and discriminator try to beat each other as the generator tries to "fool" the discriminator into believing the generated image is equivalent to ground truth. GANs can be used for a variety of medical applications such as the denoising of CT imaging, conversion of CT to MRI (or vice versa), and even segmentation.

There are several other networks out there that are used for medical tasks (such as UNet and Siamese networks); however, they all operate on the same basic concepts or aim to accomplish the same tasks as previous sections have covered (UNet is optimal for segmentation, and Siamese networks are good for image classification).

With that, we have finished our tour of ML algorithms and neural networks. Before we actually go to code these networks, let's also take some time to discuss basics of how we evaluate these networks and key steps we can do to make sure that the results we report are valid.

Other Topics
Evaluation Metrics

To provide interpretable results of the network, we have to report certain evaluation metrics to ensure the reader of our study that a network actually works as intended.

In terms of regression metrics, the most common way to report evaluation metrics is to report the mean absolute error (which is just the absolute value of the difference between the predicted number and the ground-truth number, averaged across all test instances). However, some medical journals expect you to provide a mean squared error (MSE) which penalizes a prediction that was further away from the actual value and doesn't penalize one that was very close since we square the difference between the predicted and actual values (a variation on this is the "root mean squared error" which just takes the square root of the mean squared error).

In terms of classification metrics, the simplest one is accuracy; however, that does not paint the entire picture. Often ML algorithms output a probability of something being in a particular class along with each prediction. If you have a probability, you can generate an ROC curve (as discussed earlier) and also report the area under the curve (the AUC). You can also report precision (true positive divided by true positive + false positive) or an F1 score (

$$F1 = 2 * \frac{\text{precision} * \text{recall}}{\text{precision} + \text{recall}}$$

).

You may also need to provide a calibration curve to show where the algorithm overforecasts and underforecasts probabilities of something being a particular class. These curves are made by splitting the x axis up into a fixed number of bins for the possible predicted probabilities that something belongs to a particular class (this comes out of your predictive algorithm). The value on the y axis corresponds to the number of times that the class was predicted correctly. For example, if we had 100 tested data points, we can split up their predicted probabilities on the x axis into 5 segments (predicted probability < 0.20, 0.20–0.39, 0.40–0.59, 0.60–0.79, 0.80–1). For each of the test points that produce a probability that falls into one of the bins, we also count the frequency of the true class of that test point being present. Specifically, in the first bin, we would expect a 20% of points to have the true class (since the algorithm predicted these points would have a probability of 0.20). For the next bin, it would be 40%

of points, etc. We plot the proportion of true instances of a class in a given bucket on the y axis. In the case that the model is predicting probabilities that are too large, we would see a value to the far right on the x axis but with a low y value (since, in reality, there weren't that many classes). Conversely, if the model is predicting probabilities that are too small, we would see a value to the left-hand side of the x axis, but with a high y value. An example of calibration curves can be found in Figure 4-16.

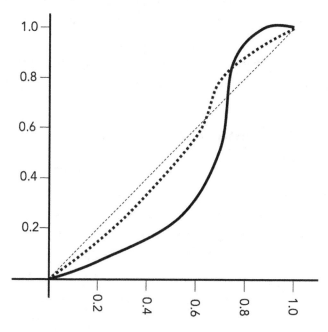

Figure 4-16. *Calibration curves. The light dashed line is a perfectly calibrated predictor. The thick solid curve is not well calibrated and the dashed thick line is a relatively well-calibrated curve*

In this image, the solid curve is underpredicting probabilities for low value probability bins and overpredicting probabilities for high value probability bins (we judge against the y=x line). There are separate methods (such as "Platt's method" which fits a logistic regression to the uncalibrated probabilities) that you can use to calibrate these uncalibrated values (ultimately producing the heavy dashed curve which "hugs" the diagonal line; here, the light dashed line is a perfectly calibrated predictor).

In general, the statistics you report are going highly dependent on the ultimate task you seek to achieve. In classification tasks, the accuracy may be sufficient to report, but medical journals would also want to see an ROC/AUC to confirm the resilience of your algorithm. Sometimes you would definitely want to see the sensitivity and specificity to get a sense for how the algorithm handles true positive, false positive, true negative, and false negative cases. It is always best to step back and figure out what someone using your model would need to know before using it. Fortunately, machine learning libraries produce a number of statistics for use and can even generate some graphs for you.

k-Fold Cross Validation

In the prior chapter, we've talked about partitioning your training set into a training set and validation set. However, we could still be fooling ourselves as to the performance of an algorithm in this case, especially if we continually try out multiple algorithms on the same training set. For all we know, the training set and validation set we initially partitioned may be something comparatively "easier" to learn compared to the real-life data.

To solve this potential issue, we can train our algorithms and validate multiple times, but on different subsets of the data. We can do so as follows: (1) Split the data into "k" number of segments (called folds), where k is a number you input (usually 5 or 10 is sufficient). (2) Pick k-1 folds of data to use as training data. (3) Train your algorithm. (4) Use the remaining fold as your validation data. (5) Keep track of evaluation metrics. (6) Continue doing steps 2 through 5, picking a different set of folds in step 2 to use for training.

Figure 4-17 illustrates how training and validation folds are usually picked in each iteration of k-fold cross validation.

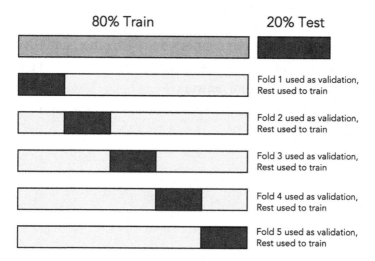

5-fold cross validation (w/test set hold out)

Figure 4-17. *5-fold cross validation is depicted in this image. 20% of the dataset is held out for testing. The remaining 80% training data is split into five folds and each fold serves as a validation fold at least once*

At the end, you can use the average of whatever evaluation metric you're interested in to compare various algorithms or hyperparameter choices. Some libraries will even allow you to do a grid search (i.e., try out many possible combinations of hyperparameters) with cross validation to provide a rigorous set of possibilities to try out.

Next Steps

In this section, we covered a number of different machine learning algorithms and saw what algorithms worked for what sorts of data/tasks. Supervised algorithms are probably the most used in medical literature since we are often trying to determine whether an algorithm matches a physician's determination of a diagnosis or not, but unsupervised algorithms have their place in the medical world as well, especially in genetics studies. We then explored perceptron-based algorithms (neural networks) and saw what a deep neural network really was (just a network with many layers of perceptrons connected to each other) and covered some of the popular classes of neural network architectures out there (with a focus on convolutional neural networks).

In the following chapters, we'll see how to actually use these algorithms on datasets.

## CHAPTER 5

Project #1 Machine Learning for Predicting Hospital Admission

Welcome to your first in-depth look at machine learning and the code behind it. In this chapter, we will be working with a dataset from the National Electron Injury Surveillance System (NEISS). This dataset, encompassing emergency room visits from 2011 to 2019 on basketball-related injuries, will be used in a task to predict whether an individual is admitted or not given their age, race, sex, location where the injury occurred, body part affected, preliminary diagnoses (from triage), and size of the care center. In the process of attempting to predict admission status, we will encounter a number of issues in machine learning including how to deal with imbalanced data, how to tune hyperparameters, and how to do feature engineering.

In the first part of this chapter, we will be working with the popular machine learning library called scikit-learn to create a decision tree classifier. Then, to make our lives a bit easier, we will switch over to using another library called PyCaret which will help us try out a bunch of different

---

All supporting code for this chapter can be found at `https://github.com/Apress/Practical-AI-for-Healthcare-Professionals/tree/main/ch5`

© Abhinav Suri 2022
A. Suri, *Practical AI for Healthcare Professionals*,
https://doi.org/10.1007/978-1-4842-7780-5_5

algorithms and see which works best. Both of these libraries can be used in the Google Colab notebook environment we used back in Chapter 3.

With that roadmap in mind, let's get started!

Data Processing and Cleaning

To get started, download the NEISS dataset from `https://github.com/Apress/Practical-AI-for-Healthcare-Professionals` (NEISS.txt). You can open up this data with excel if you want to take a peek at it. There's also an associated codebook `https://github.com/Apress/Practical-AI-for-Healthcare-Professionals` (NEISS_FMT.txt) that outlines what the values for specific variable types mean.

Our overall task is to determine what would make someone a likely admission to the hospital (this is the "Disposition" column in the file). Thinking of the potential predictors we could use, it is possible that age, sex, and race could contribute to one's admission status. Perhaps the body part injured, the location where the injury occurred, and the initial diagnosis would contribute more significantly toward the outcome. Additionally, factors such as whether there was fire involved or not and the stratum of the hospital (small, medium, large, very large) could affect the outcome.

With those factors in mind, let's get started with processing our data into something that can be used in the pandas library we used at the end of Chapter 3.

In a new Colab notebook, do the following: (1) Create a new Colab notebook. (2) Under the "Runtime" menu, select "Change Runtime Type," and then under the "Hardware Accelerator" option that pops up, select either GPU or TPU (if the TPU option is available to you). These two processors typically outperform CPUs when running tasks on training sets, getting us quicker results. (3) Upload the NEISS.txt file that was linked earlier into the folder (just like we uploaded input.csv back in Chapter 3).

Installing + Importing Libraries

In the first cell of the Colab notebook, you will need to install the following:
INPUT[CELL=1]

```
!pip install --upgrade scikit-learn catboost xgboost pycaret
```

Note   For the remainder of the chapter, anything that actually goes into your codebase will be prepended with "INPUT[CELL=Numbered cell]"; otherwise, it will be just prepended with "INPUT" or nothing at all. If you see the INPUT sign, that is also a cue to actually run the cell as well!

The output will look like a bunch of text; however, if it gives you an option at the end to "restart runtime," do it. This line basically installs upgraded versions of scikit-learn and PyCaret (both of which are Python libraries available for free); however, Colab already has some versions of those built it, meaning that it needs to reload to register their installation. (Note, in the process of restarting the Colab notebook, you will lose any variables that you have made. This is akin to starting over, just with some new dependencies).

Next, we need to import some libraries (just as we did for pandas in Chapter 3). Python libraries get imported with the following rough syntax:

```
import libraryX
import libraryX as foo
from libraryX import subFunctionY, Z
from libraryX import blah as bar
from libraryX import *
```

Let's go through this example set of import statements. The first line will import the library called "libraryX" and give you the ability to access any submodules (think of this as parts of the library) just by using the dot operator (e.g., `libraryX.someFunction`). The second line would simply give you the ability to rename `libraryX` to `foo` in case it gets tiresome to type out the full name of the library. The third line gives you the ability to only get specific parts of the library of interest (in this case `subFunctionY` and `Z`). The fourth line does the same as the combination of the second and third line. It gives you the ability to import some subcomponent of the main library and rename it. The fourth function gives you the ability to import all of the parts of the library into the namespace. In this case, you will be able to access all of the function of that library without needing to prepend it with `libraryX`. (this is useful when you're only working with one library, but don't quite know the specific parts you want to use/will be using a lot of parts from the library).

To start, we will import scikit-learn, pandas, numpy, and matplotlib:

INPUT[CELL=2]

```
import sklearn
import pandas as pd
import numpy as np
import matplotlib.pyplot as plt
```

These libraries handle the following. `sklearn` is scikit-learn and that holds many functions related to machine learning in Python. `pandas` (which we will refer to as `pd` in our code since we used the `as` keyword when importing it) allows us to manipulate and import data. `numpy` allows us to work with column- or array-based data (and give us the ability to do some basic statistics). `matplotlib` is a plotting library in Python. We will import the `pyplot` submodule under the name `plt` to create some graphs.

Reading in Data and Isolating Columns

Next, we will actually read in our data:

INPUT[CELL=3]

```
df = pd.read_csv('NEISS.TXT', delimiter='\t')
```

If you were to look at the NEISS.txt file (refer to Figure 5-1), you would see that it actually has a bunch of columns that are all separated by tab characters. Normally the pandas (here pd) read_csv function assumes that the default separator between columns (a.k.a. the delimiter) is a ,. However, in this case, we need to specify that it is tab delimited which we can do by specifying a named parameter called "delimiter" with the value \t (which is a tab character).

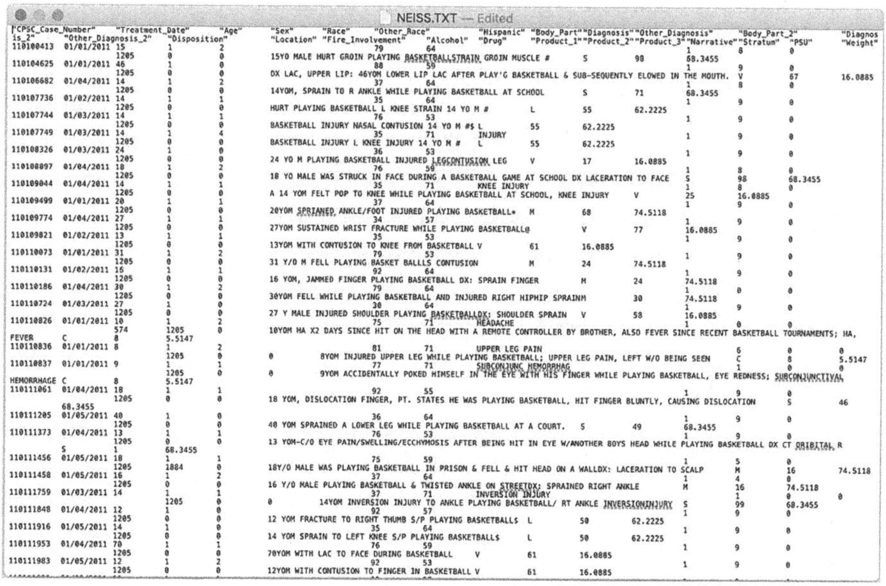

Figure 5-1. *Screenshot of the NEISS data. Note how data columns are separated by tab characters*

Side Note: Named parameters (a.k.a. "keyword arguments") allow you to specify the name of the parameter you want to give a value for when calling a method. This is particularly useful when you are calling a method that has many parameters in it. For example, if we have a function defined as follows:

```
def calculate_bmi(height, weight):
    # insert logic for calculating bmi here
```

We could call it using `calculate_bmi(1.76,64)`
(to represent getting the BMI of someone who is
1.76 m tall and 64kg), or we could say `calculate_`
`bmi(height=1.76, weight=64)` or `calculate_`
`bmi(1.76, weight=64)`. Note, we cannot say
`calculate_bmi(weight=64, 1.75)` since Python
only allows named keyword arguments to come
after non-named arguments. In the pandas read_csv
method, there are a number of parameters which
take on default values (these are parameters that
have a value automatically assumed to be equal to
something unless you specify otherwise), so having
named parameters is a time saver since you don't
have to manually specify all the parameters needed
to call the function and can selectively change the
values you pass in for the parameters you do want to
modify.

The next thing to worry about is how to actually isolate the columns we
want to look at. We can do that using the following statement:

INPUT[CELL=4]

```
df_smaller = df[['Age', 'Sex', 'Race',
'Body_Part', 'Diagnosis', 'Disposition',
'Fire_Involvement', 'Stratum', 'Location']]

# display the table so we can be sure it is what we want
print(df_smaller)
```

Upon running this cell, you should see a table with the column names
equivalent to those specified.

The first line of this code involves the selection of the columns we want
to use in our prediction task. Given that we have already stored the NEISS
data in a variable called df, we can select the columns we want by doing

df[list of columns]. In this case, the list of columns is 'Age,' 'Sex,' 'Race,' etc. We then store this result into the variable df_smaller and call display (which is a Google Colab-specific function that helps us view our pandas data).

Data Visualization

Next, we should try and visualize some of our data to determine what is actually in it. We can use the library matplotlib to help us do this. In our dataset, we have age which is a continuous variable. The rest of the data are categorical (even though they may be represented as numbers in the coding scheme they used in this dataset).

Let's go ahead and create a graph for every variable to help visualize the distribution of data:

INPUT[CELL=5]

```
fig = plt.figure(figsize=(15,10))
fig.subplots_adjust(hspace=0.4, wspace=0.4)
for idx, d in enumerate(df_smaller.columns):
  fig.add_subplot(3,3,idx+1)
  if d == 'Age':
    df[d].plot(kind='hist', bins=100, title=d)
  else:
    df[d].value_counts().plot(kind='bar', title=d)
```

OUTPUT

Refer to Figure 5-2.

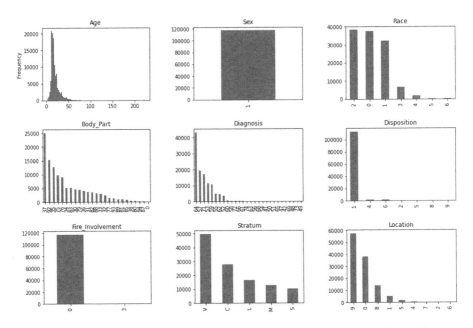

Figure 5-2. *Data visualization of various characteristics from the*
original dataset

We can see our age distribution primarily skews toward younger
people in their 20s. The sex distribution is just males (1 = male in the
NEISS codebook). Race is led by a category #2 (Black/African American).
Body_Part (which indicates the Body_Part that was injured) is led by "37"
which is ankle. Diagnosis is led by "64" which is a strain/sprain (which is to
be expected). Disposition (which is the variable that we want to predict) is
led by category "1" which indicates that the patient was treated, examined,
and released. We're trying to predict whether the patient was admitted/if
there was an adverse event that occurred which are codes 4,5, and 8. Fire_
involvement (which codes if there was any fire department involvement
with the incident) is 0 for the majority of patients (i.e., no fire department
involvement) but 3 for a very small amount of patients (possible fire
department involvement). The stratum of the hospital at which the patient
was seen is mostly very large hospitals ("V"). The Age distribution is
primarily skewed toward the lower end of the spectrum.

Digging into the code here, the first line tells matplotlib to start the creation of a figure (matplotlib figures contain multiple subplots). Note, we refer to the plotting part of matplotlib with the short name plt as we covered in the import code block and explanation. The figsize argument specifies the width and height in inches (since these figures can be output for publications, matplotlib uses inches instead of pixels to indicate widths and heights of figures).

In the second line, we adjust the spacing between subplots. This method changes the amount of padding along the width of the figure (wspace) and height of the figure (hspace). This basically states that the subplots will have padding between them (the value 0.4 means that the padding will be equivalent to 40% of the average plot's width or height).

Next, we get into a for loop. We are looping over each of the columns in the data frame we just created that contains the age, sex, etc., columns. Recall, when we use enumerate in our for loop syntax, we are going to get the value the loop is currently on (in this case the column name) stored in a variable (here, that variable is d), and we also get where the for loop is in the process of looping (stored in the index variable idx, remember this is just a number).

For each iteration of the loop, we will add a subplot with the fig. add_subplot method. This takes in the size of the subplot grid we want to create (in this case a 3x3 grid since we have nine columns) and the numbered position we want to put a plot in (which will be the idx variable plus 1 since matplotlib numbers subplots starting from 1 instead of 0). Now a subplot is created and will be filled by whatever is plotted next.

In the if else statement, we want to handle graphing different plots since our data is not the same for all columns. Age is a continuous variable and is best plotted in a histogram. Categorical data (which is all of our other columns) is best represented in a bar graph. In the if statement, we check to see if the column name (stored in d) is equal to 'Age'. If it is, then we will plot a histogram using the plotting methods that conveniently come along with our data frame. We first will grab the current column using df[d] (gets the column with name d) and then call df[d].plot and pass in the kind of plot we want ('hist' since it is a histogram), a bins argument (which specifies how fine-grained we want our histogram; here, we set it to 100), and a title for the plot (which is just the column name d that we can assign to the title named parameter).

We do the same thing for the case when we fail the if statement and enter the else branch. Here, we will need to call df[d].value_counts() to get the number of times each category appears in the dataset. We can then call .plot on that result and specify the kind as a bar graph (using kind='bar') and also show the title of the graph (similar to before).

At the end, we should get nine nice-looking graphs. In retrospect, it is definitely possible for us to eliminate the "sex" category since everyone has the same sex in our dataset and it cannot possibly provide us any way to differentiate people on that category.

Cleaning Data

Next, we need to do some data cleaning to change our Disposition column to be a binary variable (i.e., admitted vs. not admitted). First, we will need to remove all entries with the number 9 assigned as the disposition since those are unknown/no data values. Next, we will have to set all disposition values that are 4,5, or 8 as 'admit's and anything else as 'notadmit's. Let's take a look at how to do that in this code:

INPUT[CELL=6]

```
df_smaller.loc[df_smaller.Disposition == 9, 'Disposition'] =
np.nan
df_smaller['Disposition'] = df_smaller['Disposition'].dropna()

# recode individuals admitted as "admit" and those not admitted
as "notadmit"
```

```
df_smaller.loc[~df_smaller.Disposition.isin([4,5,8]),
'Disposition'] = 'notadmit'
df_smaller.loc[df_smaller.Disposition.isin([4,5,8]),
'Disposition'] = 'admit'
df_smaller['Disposition'].value_counts()
```

OUTPUT

There will be a bunch of messages saying "A value is trying to be set on a copy of a slice from a DataFrame," but at the end, you should see the following:

```
notadmit     115065
admit          2045
Name: Disposition, dtype: int64
```

It looks like we have a bunch of new syntax here. Let's dive into the code line by line.

Our first task is to get rid of any rows containing a disposition value of 9 (unknown data). We can do that by first locating any rows that have 9 in that column, setting those values equal to NaN (not a number), and then dropping (i.e., removing) any row with NaN values. Let's see how that's done with code:

```
df_smaller.loc[df_smaller.Disposition == 9, 'Disposition'] =
np.nan
df_smaller['Disposition'] = df_smaller['Disposition'].dropna()
```

In the first line, we call the .loc method on our data frame to "locate" any rows that fit a criteria that we specify. df_smaller.loc method takes in two inputs separated by a comma: the first input is the condition that must be satisfied to find the row, and the second value is the column name to edit in the case that the condition is satisfied. On the other side of the equals sign, we specify what we want rows (which satisfy the loc condition) to be. Here, we set our condition to be df_smaller.Disposition == 9 which means that we want any rows where, in the Disposition column of data frame, the value is 9. We also will edit the Disposition column (second argument) to the value on the right side of the equals sign (np.nan which is not a number and can be used to easily remove any rows).

In the second line, all we do is that we set the Disposition column equal to the Disposition column after dropping any not a number values (which np.nan is). We do that by calling .dropna() on the column.

Next, we need to set Disposition values equal to 'admit' if they are 4,5, or 8 or 'notadmit' otherwise. We will take care of the 'notadmit' case first (think about why this has to come first).

```
df_smaller.loc[~df_smaller.Disposition.isin([4,5,8]),
'Disposition'] = 'notadmit'
```

This call to loc looks relatively similar to the previous code snippet, except we have a ~ character in our condition and the isin statement which is new. The ~ indicates a logical "NOT" (which means we want the opposite of whatever follows). The isin function tests to see if values in the specified column are in the array passed as an argument to isin (in this case, we are looking for 4,5,8). In the case that a row satisfies this condition, we will set the value for that row in the 'Disposition' column equal to 'notadmit.' In the following line of code, we do the exact opposite (just be omitting the ~) and set its value equal to 'admit.'

The last line of the code block just gives us the counts for each of the values in Disposition. At the end, you should have 2045 admits and 115065 not admits.

Dealing with Categorical Data/One-Hot Encoding

An issue to be aware of in our dataset is the presence of data that looks numerical but really isn't (since all of the coded values in columns are represented as numbers). Accordingly, some of our machine learning algorithms will "think" that the data is numerical unless we specify otherwise. This specification is important to do since there is no numerical relationship between these coded values (it might be appropriate to keep them as numbers if we knew that a higher coded number indicated a higher grade outcome, i.e., the data is ordinal).

To make sure the machine learning libraries we work with understand the categorical nature of our columns, we need to generate a "one-hot encoding" of our data. To illustrate what this process does, consider our 'Race' column. This columns has values 0,1,2,3,4,5,6, each representing a different race. To generate a one-hot encoding of our data, we will create seven new columns (titled "Race_0, Race_1, Race_2, Race_3,..., Race_6") and set the values of each of the rows equal to 1 in the column that corresponds to the original data, and 0 otherwise. For example, if we had a row where Race was "2," we would set Race_0, Race_1, Race_3, Race_4, Race_5, and Race_6 in that row all equal to 0. We would only set Race_2 equal to 1.

To make this process easier, we can just call a pandas method called get_dummies to generate these columns for us across all our categorical columns as follows:

INPUT[CELL=7]

```
categorical_cols = [
 'Sex', 'Race',
 'Body_Part', 'Diagnosis',
 'Fire_Involvement', 'Stratum']
# make dummy variables for them
df_dummy = pd.get_dummies(df_smaller, columns = categorical_
cols)

# and display at the end. Should have 117110 rows and 71
columns
display(df_dummy)
```

OUTPUT

Should be something similar to Figure 5-3.

	Age	Disposition	Weight	Sex_1	Race_0	Race_1	Race_2	Race_3	Race_4	Race_5	Race_6	Body_Part_0	Body_Part_30	Body_I
0	15	notadmit	68.3455	1	0	0	1	0	0	0	0	0	0	
1	46	notadmit	16.0885	1	1	0	0	0	0	0	0	0	0	
2	14	notadmit	68.3455	1	0	0	1	0	0	0	0	0	0	
3	14	notadmit	62.2225	1	0	1	0	0	0	0	0	0	0	
4	14	notadmit	62.2225	1	0	1	0	0	0	0	0	0	0	
...	...	...	...	...	...	...	...	...	...	...	...	...	...	
117105	13	notadmit	4.8510	1	0	0	1	0	0	0	0	0	0	
117106	16	notadmit	4.8510	1	0	1	0	0	0	0	0	0	0	
117107	14	notadmit	4.8510	1	0	0	1	0	0	0	0	0	0	
117108	17	notadmit	4.8510	1	0	0	1	0	0	0	0	0	0	
117109	14	notadmit	4.8510	1	0	1	0	0	0	0	0	0	0	

117110 rows × 71 columns

Figure 5-3. *This is the dummy-variable version of our dataset. Note how many more columns we have now*

All we needed to do in this case was call `pd.get_dummies` and pass in the data frame we wanted to generate dummy variables for (here that was `df_smaller`) and the columns which we wanted to make dummy variables for (which are all the categorical columns stored in a list under the variable `categorical_cols`). We then reassign the value of df_dummy to this new data frame and display it at the end. As you can see in the screenshot, we went from 9 columns to 71 columns since we have many columns that have tons of different categorical values in them.

Now we're ready to start doing some machine learning on this data frame.

Starting the ML Pipeline

To start off, we need to specify what columns and values are our "X" (i.e., predictor variables) and what are our "Y" (i.e., outcome) variables. We can do that through these two lines of code:

INPUT[CELL=8]

```
X = df_dummy.loc[:, df_dummy.columns != 'Disposition']
Y = df_dummy['Disposition']
```

The first line of code selects all the columns except for the Disposition column and assigns it to the variable X; the second line just assigns the values in the Disposition column to the variable Y. Pretty straightforward.

Next, we need to install and import some ML-specific libraries. One library we need to install is the imbalanced learn package which helps us use algorithms to upsample underrepresented outcomes in the training process. We can do that with the following line of code:

INPUT[CELL=9]

```
!pip install imblearn
```

Next, we import some ML-specific libraries and functions:

INPUT[CELL=10]

```
from sklearn.model_selection import train_test_split,
GridSearchCV, cross_validate
from sklearn.utils import resample
from imblearn.over_sampling import SMOTE
from collections import Counter
```

Going line by line, `train_test_split`, `GridSearchCV`, and `cross_validate` from the sklearn.model_selection module take care of (1) splitting our dataset into a training set and testing set, (2) doing grid search with cross validation, and (3) doing cross validation without grid search (respectively). The resample function from `sklearn.utils` helps us resample data (which will come in handy as we try to overrepresent our underrepresented class). Next, we will import `SMOTE` from the `imblearn.over_sampling` library. SMOTE is an algorithm that selectively oversamples the minority class in a dataset. SMOTE stands for "Synthetic

Minority Oversampling Technique," and it basically will select two data points in the minority class in your dataset, draw a "line" between them in higher dimensions, and pick a random point along the line to create a new data point belonging to the minority class. This results in the generation of new data in the minority class, resulting in a more balanced dataset. The "Counter" function allows us to quickly count frequencies of unique data points in a columns.

> **Side Note**: Why oversample in our training set? In our dataset, we only have < 2% of cases that constitute admission. It is entirely possible that we could end up with a classifier that only learns to guess that everyone should not be admitted. This would lead to a high accuracy (98%) but a very low sensitivity (i.e., high # of false negatives). If we oversample in our training set, we can somewhat guarantee that the ML algorithm has to deal with the oversampled number of training data points rather than completely ignore them.

Now, let's split up our training and testing data and oversample the minority class of our training data:

INPUT[CELL=11]

```
X_train_imbalanced, X_test, y_train_imbalanced, y_test = train_
test_split(X, Y, test_size=0.30, random_state=42)

oversample = SMOTE()
X_train, y_train = oversample.fit_resample(X_train_imbalanced,
y_train_imbalanced)

print(Counter(y_train))
print(Counter(y_test))
```

OUTPUT

```
Counter({'notadmit': 80548, 'admit': 80548})
Counter({'notadmit': 34517, 'admit': 616})
```

The first line of this function calls the `train_test_split` method which takes in the X and Y variables we created earlier and allows you to specify the size of the test set with `test_size` (a proportion) and a `random_state` which allows anyone to reproduce the same results you got (whatever value you set this to doesn't matter).

This method call results in the production of four values, the train and test X data and the train and test Y data in that order (which I store in the variables `X_train_imbalanced`, `X_test`, `y_train_imbalanced`, `y_test`).

Next, we need to convert our train imbalanced datasets to something that is actually balanced using the SMOTE oversampling method.

In the second line of this code snippet, we make a new instance of the SMOTE sampler using `SMOTE()` and assign it to the variable `oversample`. We then call the `fit_resample` method on the `oversample` variable (passing in the imbalanced X and y training data) to generate the balanced X and y training data (which we store in `X_train` and `y_train`).

Lastly, we print out the call to `Counter` on our training y and testing y data which gives us the number of notadmit and admit values in our training data (first printed line) and testing data (second printed line). In our first line, we see that the notadmit and admit classes have same number of data points, which is what we wanted (i.e., class balance). In the test set, we preserve the original distribution of data (since we want to preserve real-world conditions when evaluating it).

Training a Decision Tree Classifier

Now that we have our balanced data, we can finally train a classifier. Let's go with a decision tree classifier (this is scikit-learn's version of a classification and regression tree):

INPUT[CELL=12]

```
from sklearn import tree

scoring = ['accuracy', 'balanced_accuracy', 'precision_macro',
'recall_macro', 'roc_auc']
clf = tree.DecisionTreeClassifier(random_state=42)
scores = cross_validate(clf, X_train, y_train, scoring=scoring,
return_estimator=True)
clf = scores['estimator'][np.argmax(scores['test_recall_
macro'])]
```

In the first line, we import the tree module from scikit-learn which contains the logic for creating a decision tree. In the second line, we set a variable `scoring` equal to a list of the names of metrics we want to see in our cross-validation results (here, we are getting the accuracy, balanced accuracy, precision, recall, and AUC). In the third line, we instantiate a decision tree classifier (with `tree.DecisionTreeClassifier`) and pass in a `random_state` named argument equal to a number to ensure reproducibility. We assign this untrained DecisionTreeClassifier to the variable `clf`.

Next, we call the `cross_validate` function with the following arguments:

- The classifier which in this case is going to be `clf`
- The training dataset predictors: `X_train`
- The training dataset labels: `y_train`

- The scores we want to get for each cross-validation fold: our scoring list

- Whether or not we want to get the trained decision trees for each cross-validation folds (which we do, so we set `return_estimator` to `True`)

Calling this line will take a minute or two to run since it will be training a decision tree on our data. The results of the cross validation (and the trained models) will be stored as a dictionary in the variable `scores`.

The last line of this block will save the best-performing classifier (defined as the one that has the highest recall) in a variable `clf` so we can use it later. To access the best-performing classifier, we will select an element from the list stored under the "estimator" key of the `scores` variable (which is a dictionary). The element selected will depend on the index number that corresponds to the highest recall score (note that recall scores are stored in a list under the key `'test_recall_macro'` of the `scores` variable). We get the index of the maximum element using the numpy (accessed via the keyword np) argmax method. For example, if we found that the maximum recall score was 0.97 at the index 3 of the list of recall scores, `np.argmax` would return 3, which would set `clf` equal to the fourth element (recall we start counting from 0) of the `scores['estimator']` array.

Next, to see the average scores for accuracy, etc., from the cross validation, we can print out the training statistics:

INPUT[CELL=13]

```python
for k in scores.keys():
  if k != 'estimator':
    print(f"Train {k}: {np.mean(scores[k])}")
```

OUTPUT

```
Train fit_time: 2.1358460426330566
Train score_time: 0.9156385898590088
Train test_accuracy: 0.9815949541399911
Train test_balanced_accuracy: 0.9815949560564651
Train test_precision_macro: 0.9821185121689133
Train test_recall_macro: 0.9815949560564651
Train test_roc_auc: 0.9838134464904644
```

All the earlier code does is loop through all the keys in the scores dictionary and, if the key is not equal to estimator (which contains a list of the trained decision tree classifiers), just print out "Train" followed by the statistic we are reporting followed by the mean of the values from the scores array under the key we're currently on in the for loop iteration.

Overall, we can see that the algorithm did quite well on the training dataset, but there is a major caveat we will see later on.

Grid Searching

We could also try out multiple values for various hyperparameters and do cross validation to determine what may be the best using the function GridSearchCV as follows:

INPUT[CELL=14]

```
tree_para = {'criterion':['gini','entropy'],
            'max_depth': [1,2,4]}

clf = GridSearchCV(tree.DecisionTreeClassifier(), tree_para,
cv=5, verbose=1, n_jobs=-1)
clf.fit(X_train, y_train)
clf = clf.best_estimator_
```

We just create a dictionary with a list key equal to a list of values to try out for various hyperparameters. Here, we try out using a Gini purity function or an entropy purity function and also try out multiple values for "max depth" which tell us what is the maximum number of nodes we can come across when going down the tree.

We then create a GridSearchCV instance which will take in the following arguments:

- The classifier to fit (in this case a decision tree classifier)

- The parameters to try out (will try out all combinations of the parameters specified in tree_para)

- cv=: The number of cross-validation forms to use

- verbose=: Whether or not to output training status as it is happening

- n_jobs=: Number of processing jobs to run (-1 indicates that we should use all the processing power available to us)

Running clf.fit will actually train the classifier, and we can store the best-performing classifier at the end by setting clf equal to clf.best_estimator since that is where the best-performing classifier is stored.

Note, running the previous block takes a while to do (and you can definitely skip doing so).

Next, let's see how well our decision tree classifier actually performs.

Evaluation

First, let's see if we can take a look at a basic confusion matrix. A confusion matrix plots out the predictions organized by their true label which helps us calculate sensitivity and specificity.

INPUT[CELL=15]

```
from sklearn.metrics import plot_confusion_matrix

plot_confusion_matrix(clf, X_test, y_test, values_format = '')
```

OUTPUT

Refer to Figure 5-4.

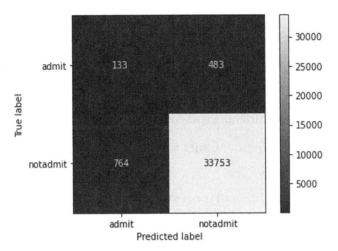

Figure 5-4. *This shows the confusion matrix from the decision tree classifier*

The code itself is pretty straightforward. We first import the plot_ confusion_matrix function from the scikit-learn matrix module. Then we call the function, passing in the trained classifier (stored in clf), the test predictors (X_test), the test labels (y_test), and a named parameter indicating that we should print out the full numbers rather than the default scientific notation (just specified using empty string ' ').

We can see here that our classifier didn't do so well as we thought. The sensitivity is 133/(133+483) = 0.215. The specificity is 33753/(33753 + 764) = 0.977 (look back at sensitivity and specificity formulas to see how we got these numbers from the confusion matrix). Since the sensitivity is so low, we can't trust this classifier to catch all the "positive" events that happen in our dataset (where "positive" means admission status) since it only gets roughly 1/5 admission decisions correct if the patient truly does need to be admitted.

But, what's the issue here? Didn't we see earlier that our training cross-validation scores were pretty close to 1 for recall (which is the same as sensitivity)? Well, it looks like our scoring function may have thought that the "notadmit" class was the "positive" class (if we recalculate using that criteria, we get a sensitivity close to 0.98).

Let's dive deeper into these evaluation metrics:

INPUT[CELL=16]

```
from sklearn.metrics import classification_report,
plot_roc_curve

y_pred = clf.predict(X_test)

print(classification_report(y_test, y_pred))

plot_roc_curve(clf, X_test, y_test)
```

OUTPUT

	precision	recall	f1-score	support
admit	0.15	0.22	0.18	616
notadmit	0.99	0.98	0.98	34517
accuracy			0.96	35133
macro avg	0.57	0.60	0.58	35133
weighted avg	0.97	0.96	0.97	35133

Refer to Figure 5-5 for the ROC curve.

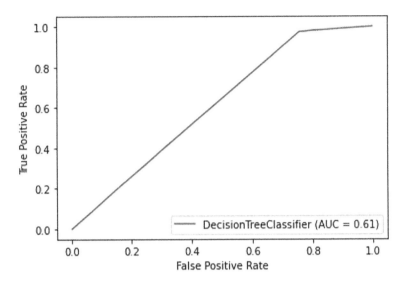

Figure 5-5. *ROC curve output from decision tree algorithm*

In the first line of code, we import methods that will help us evaluate the classification accuracy of this decision tree classifier: `classification_report` will give us a summary of important metrics for our classifier. `roc_curve` will give us the ability to do an ROC analysis on our predictions. `auc` will calculate an AUC from the ROC results. `plot_roc_curve` will plot the ROC curve.

In order to call the `classification_report` function, we need to pass in the true classifications and the predicted classifications. We get the predicted classifications by calling the `.predict` method on our trained classifier. In this case, we have stored our final trained classifier in `clf`, so we can just call `clf.predict` and pass in our test predictors (stored in `X_test`).

Next, we print out the classification report. The method that generates this report (`classification_report`) takes in the true classifications and the predicted classifications. As we can see from the results that are printed out, if we choose 'admit' to be the positive class, the recall is 0.22 (which we calculated earlier). However, if the true class is 'notadmit', the recall is 0.98 (also like we calculated earlier).

Lastly, we can plot the ROC curve by calling plot_roc_curve. This method takes in the trained classifier (clf), X_test and y_test variables. In the bottom right of the generated graph, we get the AUC which is 0.61.

Visualizing the Tree

In the case that you did run the grid search with cross validation, you may also visualize the tree (if you did not, it is unlikely that you could feasibly run the following since the tree is very complex):

INPUT[CELL=17]

```
import graphviz
if (clf.tree_.node_count < 100):
  dot_data = tree.export_graphviz(clf, out_file=None,
                                    feature_names=X.columns,
                                    class_names=['admit',
                                    'notadmit'])
  graph = graphviz.Source(dot_data)
  graph.render("neiss")
```

OUTPUT

Refer to Figure 5-6 for the output of the final tree.

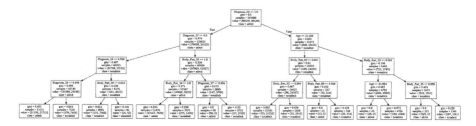

Figure 5-6. *Final tree structure output from the decision tree model we trained*

We import the graphviz library which allows us to visualize trees. Then, we check to see if there are < 100 nodes in the tree (which will be true in the case you ran the grid search since we limited the depth of the tree to be, at maximum, 4). The following lines of code are graphviz-specific lines that do not particularly mean anything of note outside of preparing the tree for exporting. Once you run the block, you'll see a file in the folder menu of Colab titled "neiss.pdf" (if you don't see it, click the folder icon on the left-hand side, and then click the folder icon with a refresh symbol on it).

Note at the bottom of tree, we see that there are several terminal boxes (called leaves). Each of these leaves has a value called a Gini coefficient. The higher this value is, the lower the purity of the leaf (meaning that this branch of the decision tree could not make a good decision as to the class of data).

This Seems Like a Lot to Do

Throughout this process, we've written dozens of lines of code, and that's just for one classifier. What if we want to try out a bunch of different classifiers? Do we have to rewrite these lines and handle the tuning/grid search ourselves? Well, maybe. However, there are several libraries out there that can help with this process. We'll explore the usage of PyCaret (a Python port of the Caret machine learning package for R).

Moving to PyCaret

PyCaret handles the process of model selection by automatically trying out a bunch of different models and giving us the ability to easily select the models we want to tune further based on whatever statistic we want to optimize (e.g., accuracy, AUC, precision, recall).

To get started, let's just import all of the classification methods in PyCaret under * so we can call them without adding the PyCaret classification submodule name in front of each method call.

We also need to change the types of our columns and adjust our output labels to work with PyCaret:

INPUT[CELL=18]

```
from pycaret.classification import *

df_smaller['Body_Part'] = df_smaller['Body_Part'].
astype('category')
df_smaller['Diagnosis'] = df_smaller['Diagnosis'].
astype('category')
df_smaller['Sex'] = df_smaller['Sex'].astype('category')
df_smaller['Race'] = df_smaller['Race'].astype('category')
df_smaller['Fire_Involvement'] = df_smaller['Fire_
Involvement'].astype('category')
df_smaller['Stratum'] = df_smaller['Stratum'].
astype('category')

df_smaller.loc[df_smaller.Disposition == 'admit',
'Disposition'] = 1
df_smaller.loc[df_smaller.Disposition == 'notadmit',
'Disposition'] = 0

print(Counter(df_smaller['Disposition']))
```

OUTPUT

```
Counter({'1': 2045, '0': 115065})
```

The first line imports all of the classification-related methods in PyCaret into the main namespace (allowing us to directly access them). The following two lines set the type of the categorical columns (Body_Part, Diagnosis, etc.) to 'category' using the .astype modifier on data frames. We assign the resulting transformation back to the original column type.

We also need to change the 'admit' and 'notadmit' variables in our 'Disposition' column to either a 1 or 0 (where 1 is the positive class). We've used this syntax before, but if it is unfamiliar, go back up when we originally processed the dataset.

Next, we need to set up a PyCaret experiment:

INPUT[CELL=19]

```
grid=setup(data=df_smaller, target='Disposition', verbose=True,
fix_imbalance=True,
          bin_numeric_features=['Age'], log_experiment=True,
          experiment_name='adv1', fold=5)
```

OUTPUT

There will be an interactive component that asks you to verify the types of variables. It should look like Figure 5-7.

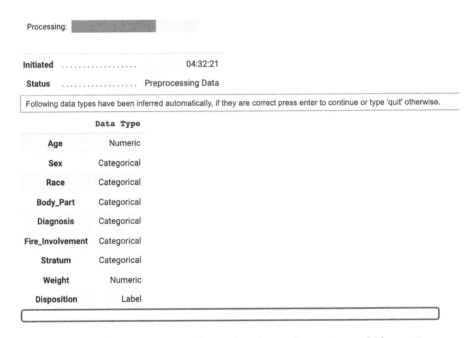

Figure 5-7. This is a screenshot of PyCaret in action while setting up the training process

Press enter and then take a look at the output. There will be a table with two columns "Description" and "Value." Make sure that the following are true:

- Target = Disposition

- Target Type = Binary

- Label Encoded = 0: 0, 1: 1

- Transformed Train Set = (81976, 101)

- Transformed Test Set = (35134, 101)

- Fold Number = 5

- Fix Imbalance Method = SMOTE

Going through the code, we call PyCaret's setup function. We pass in our data df_smaller and specify the target variable to predict Disposition. We also say that we want to see all output (with verbose=True), we want to fix any class imbalances (fix_imbalance=True), and we also want to "bin" the numeric feature Age (i.e., allocate data into individual numbered bins and learn on the b in number the raw number, which is better for some algorithms). We also want to log (i.e., record the training process) our experiment which we name 'adv1' (experiment_name='adv1'). Lastly, we specify that we only want to do fivefold cross validation (default is 10) to save some time (fold=5).

So now that we are done with setting up the PyCaret experiment, let's actually run some models:

INPUT[CELL=20]

```
topmodels = compare_models(n_select = len(models()))
```

OUTPUT

Refer to Figure 5-8.

155

Processing: ▓▓▓▓▓▓▓▓▓▓▓▓▓▓

Initiated	....	04:39:33
Status	....	Fitting 5 Folds
Estimator	....	K Neighbors Classifier

	Model	Accuracy	AUC	Recall	Prec.	F1	Kappa	MCC	TT (Sec)
lr	Logistic Regression	0.7966	0.8769	0.8244	0.0667	0.1234	0.0943	0.1974	16.604

	Model	Accuracy	AUC	Recall	Prec.	F1	Kappa	MCC	TT (Sec)
rf	Random Forest Classifier	0.9495	0.8084	0.3392	0.1314	0.1893	0.1685	0.1890	24.550
et	Extra Trees Classifier	0.9494	0.7527	0.3378	0.1304	0.1881	0.1673	0.1878	37.966
dt	Decision Tree Classifier	0.9477	0.7110	0.3518	0.1297	0.1895	0.1684	0.1912	2.810
lightgbm	Light Gradient Boosting Machine	0.9399	0.8804	0.4558	0.1355	0.2088	0.1871	0.2252	3.452
knn	K Neighbors Classifier	0.9069	0.6981	0.3631	0.0714	0.1193	0.0930	0.1287	403.662
gbc	Gradient Boosting Classifier	0.8513	0.8793	0.7219	0.0802	0.1443	0.1167	0.2070	35.166
ada	Ada Boost Classifier	0.8436	0.8725	0.7380	0.0780	0.1411	0.1133	0.2058	9.824
lr	Logistic Regression	0.7966	0.8769	0.8244	0.0667	0.1234	0.0943	0.1974	16.604
ridge	Ridge Classifier	0.7778	0.0000	0.8308	0.0618	0.1150	0.0854	0.1876	0.830
lda	Linear Discriminant Analysis	0.7778	0.8754	0.8308	0.0618	0.1150	0.0854	0.1876	4.574
svm	SVM - Linear Kernel	0.7516	0.0000	0.8490	0.0566	0.1062	0.0761	0.1783	1.904
nb	Naive Bayes	0.2774	0.6239	0.9249	0.0218	0.0426	0.0090	0.0566	0.754
qda	Quadratic Discriminant Analysis	0.0249	0.5001	0.9923	0.0174	0.0341	0.0000	-0.0026	3.328
xgboost	Extreme Gradient Boosting	0.0000	0.0000	0.0000	0.0000	0.0000	0.0000	0.0000	0.670
catboost	CatBoost Classifier	0.0000	0.0000	0.0000	0.0000	0.0000	0.0000	0.0000	0.760

Figure 5-8. *Output models from PyCaret's training process*

The training statistics for a number of ML algorithms. **NOTE:** This step will take a long time (roughly 30 minutes). Grab a cup of tea/coffee while you're waiting.

The `compare_models` method will actually run all the available models in PyCaret's library for classification. All the models available can be accessed by calling the `models()` method (there are 18 in total). We also pass in an `n_select` parameter to select the top "N" number of models, where "N" is the number we specify. Since it would be best to keep all of the trained models, we specify "N" to be number of models (which can be accessed with a `len(models())` call). We assign this to the `topmodels` variable.

156

After that is done running, we will get a list of all the models that have been trained. Note that this list will be fairly long, but it is up to you to figure out the one that would be most appropriate for the task. You should try and find a model that balances accuracy, AUC, and recall (with recall being the highest priority item to value).

For me, the best models were a gradient boosting machine (gbm), AdaBoost (ada), and logistic regression (lr). They ranked as the sixth, seventh, and eighth highest accuracy models. I can access them by indexing into the top models variable (which is just a list that stores a trained model at each index).

> **Side Note**: We've covered some of these algorithms before, but not gradient boosting machines and AdaBoost.
>
> AdaBoost is an algorithm that creates many decision trees that have a single split, that is, they just have two leaf nodes and a single decision node. These are called "decision stumps." These decision stumps each receive a vote in the process of determining the prediction. These tree votes receive a vote that is proportional to their accuracy. As the algorithm sees more training samples, it will add new decision stumps upon the algorithm encountering difficult training data points (i.e., data that doesn't lead to a strong majority). AdaBoost keeps adding decision stumps until it can handle these difficult training data points which receive a higher weight in the training process (i.e., are "higher priority" to learn correctly). Gradient boosting operates similar to AdaBoost; however, it does not assign a higher weight to difficult to learn data points. Rather it will try and optimize some loss function and iteratively add/weight

individual tree votes based on whether they minimize any loss (through a gradient descent process).

INPUT[CELL=21]

```
gbm = topmodels[5]
ada = topmodels[6]
lr = topmodels[7]
```

We can also plot various results from the each of these models using the plot_model function (which takes in the trained model as the first argument and the plot type as the second argument). Here are a couple of graphs for the gradient boosting machine:

INPUT[CELL=22]

```
plot_model(gbm, 'auc')
```

OUTPUT

Refer to Figure 5-9.

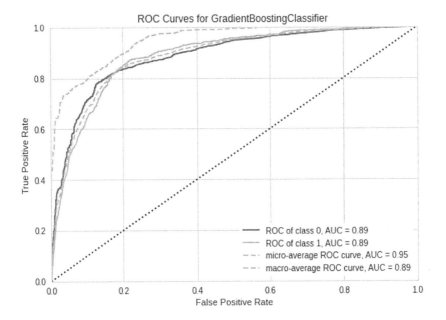

Figure 5-9. *Output AUC from PyCaret's trained GBM model*

We can see that the AUC is close to 0.89 which is great. Let's take a look at the confusion matrix:

INPUT[CELL=23]

```
plot_model(gbm, 'confusion_matrix')
```

OUTPUT

Refer to Figure 5-10.

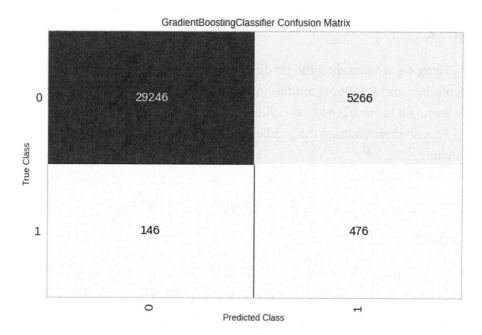

Figure 5-10. *Output confusion matrix from PyCaret's trained GBM model*

These results seem to be pretty decent. The sensitivity (a.k.a. recall) is (476/(476+146) = 0.765) which is a massive improvement over what our decision tree classifier produced.

We can even go so far as to combine multiple models together. This method (called blending) allows us to train another model that takes outputs from the component submodels and generates an output.

This effectively reduces the total feature space the blended model has
to learn on from nine columns to just the number of models you're
blending, making learning more efficient. It can also help to visualize
this as allowing each model to have a "vote" on the outcome and training
another model to learn which votes to value more/less. Let's take a look at
how to make one blended model:

INPUT[CELL=24]

```
blender = blend_models(estimator_list=[gbm, lr, ada],
method='auto')
```

Here, we are blending the gradient boosting machine, logistic
regression, and AdaBoost models together to make a blended model and
are storing it in the `blender` variable.

We can then evaluate the predictions using the `predict_model`
function:

INPUT[CELL=25]

```
predict_model(blender, probability_threshold=0.43)
```

OUTPUT

Model	Accuracy	AUC	Recall	Prec.	F1	Kappa	MCC
Voting Classifier	0.8333	0.8916	0.8135	0.081	0.1474	0.119	0.2232

Note, we can change the probability threshold at which we define
something as being a case. In this case, decreasing the probability
threshold from the default (0.5) to 0.43 leads to a higher recall (0.765 vs.
0.81) at the slight expense of accuracy (83.3% instead of 85%).

Extra: Exporting/Loading a Model

If you want to save the final model, it is as simple as doing the following:

```
save_model(insert_model_variable_here, 'modelfilename')
```

You can then find that model in your Colab file menu (refresh it if you don't see it).

Additionally you can load the model back into memory from the file by calling the following:

```
model_variable = load_model('modelfilename')
```

(Note: you would have to re-upload the model file to the Colab environment if you run this line in a separate session since Colab files do not persist).

Summary and What's Next

Over the past chapter, we've covered how to train a model from scratch in scikit-learn. We specifically explored how to configure a decision tree classifier. In the process, we also did some preliminary data exploration, cleaned our data and formatted it for use in machine learning applications, and went through the process of tuning hyperparameters for our final tree and evaluating its efficacy (and figuring out what metrics we should value more than others).

We then went on to use PyCaret to help automate the model selection process and saw how to combine multiple models together to create a blended model. For the vast majority of tabular data (i.e., data that is just a spreadsheet usually), it is much easier to start with exploring machine learning algorithms rather than attempting to code those algorithms from scratch. This fact makes it fairly straightforward to start exploring the usage of these ML algorithms in medical research and even clinical outcomes prediction (just as we did for this dataset).

161

However, machine learning algorithms typically do not work well for image-based data, mainly because it is difficult to capture location-based information within the image itself. To tackle that task, we need to take a look into convolutional neural networks which we will explore in the next chapter.

## CHAPTER 6

Project #2 CNNs and Pneumonia Detection from Chest X-Rays

Now that we've taken a look at basic machine learning algorithms and how they work, let's turn to neural networks. In this chapter, we are going to be tackling an image classification challenge: trying to use chest x-rays to detect pneumonia in patients (i.e., assign a status of "pneumonia" or "normal" to each image). We'll also see how we can visualize what the neural network "pays attention to" when evaluating images (via using a technique called "Grad-CAM").

Project Setup

To get started, we need to find a suitable dataset for this task. Luckily, a website called Kaggle regularly hosts machine learning competitions (some of which are related to medical image classification tasks). As part of these competitions, organizations (usually companies, but also governmental bodies such as the NIH) provide public datasets for usage.

All supporting code for this chapter can be found at `https://github.com/Apress/Practical-AI-for-Healthcare-Professionals/tree/main/ch6`

© Abhinav Suri 2022
A. Suri, *Practical AI for Healthcare Professionals*,
https://doi.org/10.1007/978-1-4842-7780-5_6

We'll be using the following dataset for this chapter: `www.kaggle.com/paultimothymooney/chest-xray-pneumonia`.

The relevant tasks for this project are as follows:

1. Download the dataset into a Colab notebook using the Kaggle API.

2. Split data into training, validation, and testing set and visualize the distribution of normal and pneumonia cases.

3. Create data generators (you'll find out what this is later on in the chapter) for each of our data subsets and augment our training/validation images.

4. Create a small neural network termed "SmallNet" for our image classification task.

5. Set up network "callbacks" to adjust neural network parameters during the training process and log progress statistics.

6. Train smallnet.

7. Use an existing neural network (VGG16) and customize it for our dataset (via a process known as "transfer learning").

8. Train VGG16.

9. Visualize an activation map from both models using Grad-CAM on a test set and evaluate both models.

With all of that in mind, let's get started!

Colab Setup

Make sure that you change your runtime type to a "GPU" for this chapter. In a new Colab notebook, go to Runtime ➤ Change Runtime Type, and change CPU or TPU over to GPU on the drop-down menu.

Downloading Data

First, we need to download the images that we are going to use.

We will be using this Kaggle dataset: `www.kaggle.com/ paultimothymooney/chest-xray-pneumonia`.

To quickly download the dataset, you will need to do the following:

1. Create a Kaggle.com account.

2. Click your profile picture (in the upper right-hand corner).

3. Click "Account."

4. Scroll down to the "API" section.

5. First, click "Expire API Token." Make sure that a notice pops up saying that API tokens were expired or no API tokens exist.

6. Then click "Create New API Token"; doing this should make a kaggle.json file which is automatically downloaded to your computer.

7. Upload the kaggle.json file to Google Colab.

8. Run the following lines of code:

INPUT[CELL=1]

```
!pip install kaggle
!mkdir /root/.kaggle
!cp kaggle.json /root/.kaggle/kaggle.json
!chmod 600 /root/.kaggle/kaggle.json
!kaggle datasets download -d paultimothymooney/chest-xray-pneumonia
```

```
!unzip chest-xray-pneumonia.zip
!rm -rf chest_xray/__MACOSX
!rm -rf chest_xray/chest_xray
```

OUTPUT There are many, many lines of text that aren't too relevant to describe in detail. However, let's go through what all of the above actually does.

In prior chapters, we've sometimes used the !pip install somelibrary line in our code. But what is that ! actually doing in this case? Well, commands such as pip ... aren't actually Python code. They're rather commands that you would normally feed into a command prompt or terminal (this is a separate program on your computer that allows you to access files and run scripts just by typing a few keywords). The pip install command will actually call a separate program to find a Python library from online, download it to your computer, and install it so that you can use it. Here, we're installing the kaggle Python library which allows us to interact with the kaggle.com website programmatically. But why go through all the effort of doing that when the chest x-ray challenge page has a big button that allows us to download the entire dataset? Well, that dataset is quite large (several gigabytes), and it would take a while to download to our computer. Furthermore, we would need to then upload that dataset back to the Colab notebook, which can be very time consuming. Rather, we can use the Kaggle Python library to automatically download a dataset to Colab (or wherever you are running a Python notebook).

Let's go through all of the other lines of the previous code snippet.

Line 2 will create a folder named .kaggle at the location /root/ (note, mkdir is short for "make directory" which is a handy way to remember that it is for making folders since a directory is just another name for a folder). But why should we create a folder at such a location? Kaggle's library actually requires us to store that kaggle.json file (we downloaded from their website) inside of the /root file under the .kaggle subfolder. Also, a minor side note: the /root folder is a folder that is present at the system level. Most of the folders that you interact with are present at the user level (e.g., Desktop, Downloads, Photos, etc.).

Line 3 copies the kaggle.json file we have in the Colab main directory to the .kaggle subfolder of the /root folder. It also makes sure that its name is still kaggle.json in that location. Notice how we specify locations in these commands as folder/subfoldername/subsubfoldername/. These are called file paths and are convenient ways of referring to specific locations rather than continually mentioning something is a subfolder of another folder. Also note, cp is short for copy (also an easier way to remember it).

Line 4 alters the "permissions" of the kaggle.json file. File permissions are system-level restrictions that allow us to specify exactly what a user can and can't do with a typical file. Here, we set the file permissions of the kaggle.json file to be 600 which means that it can be read from and written to. We won't be doing any writing to the file itself, but it's just nice to keep it there in case you would ever need to edit the file directly.

Line 5 will call the Kaggle library command line tool (the part of the Kaggle library that can be interacted with from the command line rather than a Python program) and will download the dataset matching the name paultimothymooney/chest-xray-pneumonia (note the -d in the full command is used to specify that the files associated with the dataset should be downloaded).

Line 6 is used to unzip the zip file that was downloaded in the prior step. This will lead to the creation of a chest_xray folder in the main Colab directory.

Lines 7 and 8 remove two subfolders called __MACOSX and chest_xray in the chest_xray folder. The contents of these subfolders contain copies of the main dataset anyway, so it is unnecessary to keep storing them in our Colab session.

Splitting Data

At the end of running these commands, you should have a folder called "chest_xray" with three subfolders called "test," "train," and "val." If you attempt to look at the individual folders, you'll see that the "train" folder has two subfolders called "NORMAL" and "PNEUMONIA" (same with "val" and "test"). The train NORMAL and PNEUMONIA folders have many images (.jpg files) and so does the test folder. However, the "val" folder only has a few images in both of the NORMAL and PNEUMONIA folder. These folders contain the training, validation, and test data for training our neural network; however, since there is so little validation data (only 16 images), it would be best for us to try and re-split the data ourselves to ensure a better split between training, validation, and test data.

To do so, we'll basically do the following:

1. Get the paths (a.k.a. file locations) of all of the images in the chest_xrays folder.

2. Re-split the data so that 20% of it is used for testing.

3. Verify we did things correctly and didn't disturb the distribution of data by plotting the frequency of normal vs. pneumonia images in the training dataset and testing dataset.

So that should take care of making sure that our train/test split is adequate. We'll handle how to make a validation split later on, but let's see the code:

INPUT[CELL=2]

```
import numpy as np
import matplotlib.pyplot as plt
import pandas as pd
from imutils import paths
from sklearn.model_selection import train_test_split
```

```
def generate_dataframe(directory):
  img_paths = list(paths.list_images(directory))
  labels = ['normal' if x.find('NORMAL') > -1 else 'pn' for x
  in img_paths]
  return pd.DataFrame({ 'paths': img_paths, 'labels': labels })

all_df = generate_dataframe('chest_xray')

train, test = train_test_split(all_df, test_size=0.2, random_
state=42)

print(train['labels'].value_counts())
print(test['labels'].value_counts())
```

OUTPUT

```
pn        3419
normal    1265
Name: labels, dtype: int32
pn        854
normal    318
Name: labels, dtype: int32
```

The first five lines of code are just used to import some libraries that will help us for this task (and others down the road). There is one new library we haven't seen before called imutils. It is used for handling images and provides a handy module called paths that will find all of the images within a folder (and all of its subfolders). This will be very useful in getting us a list of all the images.

In general, the code is structured so that we first call a method we define called generate_dataframe. This makes a pandas data frame that contains two columns: one with the paths to all the images and the other column saying what is the label of that image (normal or pneumonia).

169

Then we will split that data using the `train_test_split` method from scikit-learn and specify that we want 20% of our data to be allocated to the test set. Lastly, we'll print out the count of each class in the training and testing set we just generated. Let's take a further look at the `generate_dataframe` method since that one is not something we've encountered before.

The `generate_dataframe` method takes in a single argument called `directory`. This gets passed to the `paths.list_images` method which returns to us as a Python generator (you don't really need to know what this is other than the fact that it can make a function that behaves like a for loop). However, we don't really want a generator; we just want a list of the file paths. To get that, we simply wrap the `paths.list_images` call in a `list()` call, and that returns our image paths containing all of the images in all of the subfolders of the directory we called `generate_dataframe` with.

Next, we need to find the actual labels associated with each of these images. As mentioned earlier, each image lives within a folder named either NORMAL or PNEUMONIA. So, all we need to do is look in each of our image paths and see if the word "NORMAL" appears: if it does, it is a normal image; otherwise, it is a pneumonia image. We can do that by using a list comprehension:

```
['normal' if x.find('NORMAL') > -1 else 'pn' for x in img_paths]
```

which is basically the equivalent of

```
new_list = []
for x in img_paths:
    if x.find('NORMAL') > -1
        new_list.append('normal')
    else:
        new_list.append('pn')
```

A small reminder: the .find function on the string file path (temporarily stored in the variable x) will return -1 if the phrase passed to .find is not found; otherwise, it returns something greater than -1.

At this point, we now have a list of image paths, and we have a list of labels. It would be nice to have this in a data frame with two columns (one for paths and one for labels) since it works well with other methods in the library we will use to build our neural networks. To do that, all we need to do is call the pd.DataFrame method and pass in a dictionary with keys equivalent to the column names and respective values equal to the lists making up those columns.

We can then call generate_dataframe('chest_xray') to get a data frame of all of the images. The train_test_split method will split up our data frame as well (and will try to ensure that both classes have the same distribution of labels). Lastly, we will print out the frequency of labels in the newly generated train and test data frames by calling .value_counts() on the 'labels' column for each.

We can continue by plotting out the counts as well:

INPUT[CELL=3]

```
fig = plt.figure(figsize=(10,3))
for idx, x in enumerate([train, test]):
  fig.add_subplot(1,2,idx+1)
  x['labels'].value_counts().plot(kind='bar')
```

OUTPUT

Refer to Figure 6-1.

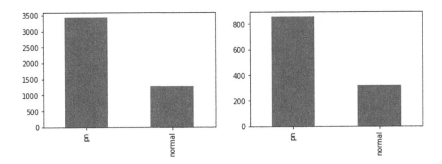

Figure 6-1. *Distribution of training and test cases*

We can see here that the distribution of normal vs. pneumonia (here called "pn") images in the train and test datasets is basically the same. Importantly, we see that pneumonia data is overrepresented relative to the normal data which could bias our network if we don't account for that.

Now that we have our training and test datasets created, we can get started with actually working with the neural network building library tensorflow and keras (which is contained within TensorFlow). We'll first get started by creating an ImageDataGenerator that allows the network to easily get training, validation, and testing images.

Creating Data Generators and Augmenting Images

Data generators are the way that our network can actually use the training and test data we have stored in our data frames. Since our data frame only contains the path to the image and the label, we would ideally like some way of automatically reading those images into the computer's memory so that our soon-to-be-made neural network program can actually learn on it (or be evaluated on images).

The neural network libraries we are using give us the ability to create an ImageDataGenerator which will allow us to specify data augmentations (random transformations to our images that provide us the ability to

172

continually generate images that are all unique rather than training on the exact same images) and give us the ability to specify a data frame from which to load images from.

> **Side Note**: Why do we need to augment our images? The way that the neural network trains is that it goes through all of the training images one time (usually in groups of images called "batches"). Each training run over the entire imaging set is called an "epoch." Some neural networks will need multiple epochs to actually train to a point that is viable for real-world usage, but training on the same images again and again runs the risk of overfitting to your training data. We can use the ImageDataGenerator to randomly alter the source training images for each epoch. We can specify random transformations to the image (called "augmentations") such as rotating it by a certain maximum number of degrees, flipping it horizontally, shifting it left/right, or changing its brightness. We'll use some of these augmentations in our scripts.

Let's set up a method that allows us to create all of the generators we need (i.e., training, validation, and test generators).

INPUT[CELL=4]

```
from tensorflow.keras.preprocessing.image import
ImageDataGenerator

def create_generators(train, test, size=224, b=32):
  train_generator = ImageDataGenerator(
      rescale=1./255, rotation_range=5, width_shift_range=0.1,
      height_shift_range=0.1, validation_split=0.2
```

```
)
test_generator = ImageDataGenerator(rescale=1./255)

baseargs = {
    "x_col": 'paths',
    "y_col": 'labels',
    "class_labels": ['normal', 'pn'],
    "class_mode": 'binary',
    "target_size": (size,size),
    "batch_size": b,
    "seed": 42
}
train_generator_flow = train_generator.flow_from_dataframe(
  **baseargs,
  dataframe=train,
  subset='training')
validation_generator_flow = train_generator.flow_from_
dataframe(
  **baseargs,
  dataframe=train,
  subset='validation')
test_generator_flow = test_generator.flow_from_dataframe(
    **baseargs,
    dataframe=test,
    shuffle=False)

return train_generator_flow, validation_generator_flow,
test_generator_flow
```

OUTPUT

There won't be any output since we're just defining a method here. We'll call it after we go through what it does.

Here, we define a method called `create_generators` that takes in our train and test sets. We also specify two other arguments `size=224, b=32`. These are "default named arguments" (they function as normal arguments but will only have the specified value unless the method call specifies otherwise). `size` and `b` will be used to dictate how the images should be resized and what is the "batch size" (i.e., the number of images a neural network will see at each training step of the epoch) for each generator.

Next, we create two instances of the `ImageDataGenerator`, a training image data generator and a testing image data generator. In the training image data generator, we specify a number of arguments as follows:

- `rescale` is a number multiplied by each pixel in the image. We set this equal to `1./255` which just means that we multiply everything by 1/255. That number was chosen because most neural network architectures are scale sensitive, meaning that it becomes difficult for a network to learn on the full range of pixel values (0–255). Instead, we can rescale our image pixels to values between 0 and 1 (which multiplying the entire image by 1/255 does).

- `rotation_range` is the first augmentation parameter we have. Since we have it set equal to 5, we will randomly rotate each image by anywhere between 0 and 5 degrees in the clockwise or counterclockwise direction.

- `width_shift_range` and `height_shift_range` are the second and third augmentation parameters. They shift the image width and height by 0–10% (0.1) of the image width and height, respectively.

- validation_split is the parameter that splits up our
  training set into a training set and a testing set. Since
  we have its value specified as 0.2, 20% of what we
  originally defined as the training set will be allocated to
  a validation subset.

For the test image data generator, we only need to rescale our
image (since we want to test on actual images without any additional
transformations).

Instantiating an ImageDataGenerator object isn't enough to actually
get the data generator to read images from our data frames. To do that,
we have to call .flow_from_dataframe on each of data generators we
currently have (a train and test data generator). With that, let's dive into the
second segment of the earlier code:

```
...
  baseargs = {
      "x_col": 'paths',
      "y_col": 'labels',
      "class_labels": ['normal', 'pn'],
      "class_mode": 'binary',
      "target_size": (size,size),
      "batch_size": b,
      "seed": 42
  }
  train_generator_flow = train_generator.flow_from_dataframe(
    **baseargs,
    dataframe=train,
    subset='training')
...
```

Here, we've defined a dict that has multiple keys and values. This dict
is then passed to our function but is represented as **baseargs. What does
the ** do? It actually expands out our dictionary into named arguments so

176

that each key and value of the dictionary is a named argument name and value. So the earlier example is the equivalent of saying

```
train_generator_flow = train_generator.flow_from_dataframe(
    x_col='paths',
    y_col='labels',
    class_labels=['normal', 'pn'],
    class_mode='binary',
    target_size=(size,size),
    batch_size=b,
    dataframe=train,
    subset='training')
```

It's just a little bit more convenient to use the ** syntax since we will be repeating these parameters across each of the generators.

Each of the arguments does the following:

- dataframe specifies what the source data frame is that contains the data for where the images are located and their associated labels.

- We also need to specify which column contains the image path (x_col argument) and which one contains the label (y_col argument).

- Additionally, we need to specify the class labels (argument class_labels) as a list (note: class names get internally converted to a 0 or 1, the first element of the list will be treated as a 0, and the second element will be a 1).

- Since we are only dealing with two categories to predict, we can specify the outcome (via the class_ mode argument) should be treated as a binary variable (if we're predicting multiple things, we can use categorical as the class_mode).

- We also can also resize our images to a width and height specified in a tuple as the argument to target_size. Here, we've set size equal to 224, meaning we'll feed 224px x 224px images into our neural network (this will become important later on).

- We also set the batch size (i.e., the number of images we present to the neural network at once) via the batch_size variable. We're setting the batch size to 32, but this can be as small or as large as you want (larger batch sizes take up more memory, smaller batch sizes take up less memory, but could cause the network to learn slower since it only sees one image at a time before updating its weights).

- Additionally, for the training and validation generators we make, we can specify what subset of the data to select from. Recall that when we made the ImageDataGenerator stored in the train_generator variable, we specified a validation split of 0.2. This allocates 80% of the data frame rows to the training subset and 20% to the validation subset. Since we're making a fully "flowed" training generator, we want to select the training subset of this training generator, which we can do with the subset argument.

- Lastly, we can ensure reproducibility of the data splits by specifying a "seed" argument (this is just equal to a random number, but anyone who runs flow from data frame with this number should get the same split of images we do).

We store the train_generator that has had .flow_from_dataframe called on it in the train_generator_flow variable.

We also set up the "flowed" validation generator similar to the "flowed" train generator, except we specify the subset to be the 'validation' subset of the original train generator.

Lastly, we set up the "flowed" test generator similar to the other two, except we don't include the subset argument and set the source data frame as the test data frame. Additionally, we disable the shuffling of images in the dataset. Normally, all of the images are shuffled on each epoch ensuring the network isn't exposed to images in the same order; however, this behavior makes it harder to evaluate images (will lead to incorrect labels being used to evaluate the image).

Now, let's see if everything worked by calling the create_generators method and displaying some images from our training generator:

INPUT[CELL=5]

```
train_generator, validation_generator, test_generator = create_
generators(train, test, 224, 32)

imgs = train_generator.next()
fig = plt.figure(figsize=(10,10))
for i in range(16):
  fig.add_subplot(4,4,i+1)
  image = imgs[0][i]
  label = 'PNEUMONIA' if imgs[1][i] == 1 else 'NORMAL'
  plt.axis('off')
  plt.imshow(image)
  plt.title(label)
```

OUTPUT

Refer to Figure 6-2.

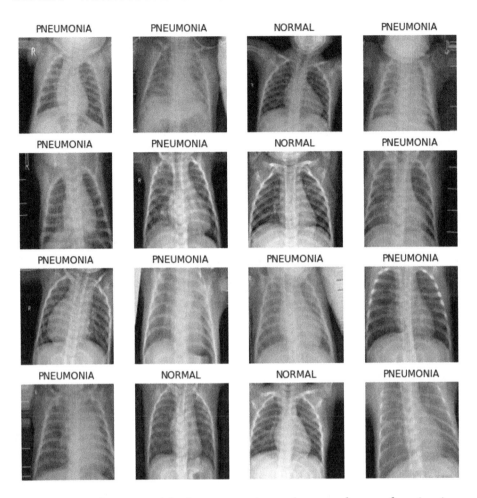

Figure 6-2. *Output grid of pneumonia and normal cases for viewing*

We first called our create_generators method with the train and test datasets as well as 224 and 32 for the image size and batch size, respectively (though we could have omitted these two arguments since they have default values in the method definition).

The next section of the code samples one batch of images from the train generator (using `train_generator.next()`) and creates a figure. We store these images in the `imgs` variable. `train_generator.next()` returns two lists: the first list contains all the images and can be accessed using `imgs[0]`; the second list contains the corresponding labels and can be accessed using `imgs[1]`.

Next, we'll display the first 16 images from this training batch (note there are 32 images in the batch overall).

`for i in range(16)` makes a for loop that runs 16 times (and `i` increases by 1, starting from 0). For each iteration of the for loop, we add a subplot to the image by specifying three numbers: the first two numbers define the grid of subplots (4x4 to accommodate all 16 images), and the last number specifies which number subplot (starting at 1) the image will be plotted in.

To get the image to plot, we will access the ith index training image which is stored in `imgs[0][i]`. We will also get the label of the image from `imgs[1][i]` and store its value as "PNEUMONIA" if the label is equal to 1; otherwise, it will store it as "NORMAL."

Finally, we show the image (which plots it into the subplot) using `plt.imshow` method and set the plot title with `plt.title`, passing in the label we set before.

As you can see, some of the images are slightly rotated and shifted and all seem like plausible images we may see in the test set (which is the aim of data augmentation).

Now that we've set up our data generators for use in the neural networks, let's actually specify how the neural networks are structured.

Your First Convolutional Neural Network: SmallNet

Neural networks are typically specified using the following general steps:

1. Specify the structure of the network (i.e., all of the individual layers that go into it).

2. Compile the network and specify how it learns (via an optimizer), how it's penalized for bad learning (via a loss function), and how it measures its progress (via metrics).

3. Specify callbacks which determine if anything should be recorded at the end of each epoch, when the model should be saved, and how some parameters should change.

4. Train (a.k.a. fit) the model.

The overall structure of our program will be as follows (note, this is just a rough sketch and not actual code):

```
def make_modelname():
    # specify model layers and compile model
    # return compiled model
def get_callbacks():
    # return list of callbacks
def run_model(train_generator):
    model = make_modelname()
    callbacks = get_callbacks()
    # fit the model
    model.fit(train_generator, callbacks)
```

In this section, we'll tackle steps 1 and 2. To do that, let's specify a neural network architecture we'll call "SmallNet" since it has relatively few parameters to train on. Before we do that, we need to import several methods:

INPUT[CELL=6]

```
from tensorflow.keras.models import Sequential, load_model
from tensorflow.keras.optimizers import Adam
from tensorflow.keras.layers import Dense,
GlobalAveragePooling2D, Conv2D, MaxPooling2D, Flatten, Dropout
from tensorflow.keras.callbacks import ReduceLROnPlateau,
ModelCheckpoint, TensorBoard, EarlyStopping
from tensorflow.keras.metrics import Recall, Precision, AUC
from tensorflow.keras.applications import EfficientNetB4
from tensorflow.keras.utils import plot_model
from datetime import datetime
```

- The first line imports a model type called a "Sequential" model from the Keras machine learning library. It also imports a "load_model" method we will use later when attempting to retrain a model that has been saved to disk.

- The second line imports an optimizer called "Adam." Adam will adaptively change the learning rate of the neural network so that it adjusts how quickly it adjusts its weights.

- The third line imports a variety of layers (think of these as sections to the neural network). We'll use all of these in the creation of "SmallNet."

- The fourth line imports some callback methods.
  ReduceLROnPlateau will drop the learning rate
  if the performance of the network stagnates,
  ModelCheckpoint allows us to save the network after
  the completion of each epoch, TensorBoard allows us
  to visualize the training progress of our network, and
  EarlyStopping allows us to stop the training of the
  network early if there is no improvement whatsoever
  (helps us avoid overfitting).

- The fifth line imports some metrics to monitor during
  the training of the network.

- The sixth line imports a neural network architecture
  called VGG16. We will adjust a pretrained version of this
  network to work for our task.

- The seventh line imports a method called plot_model
  which gives us the ability to visualize the structure of
  our neural network.

- The last line just gives us the ability to get the current
  date and time (we'll need this when creating logs for
  training progress).

Now that we've defined the imports we need, let's get to specifying our
"smallnet" architecture:

INPUT[CELL=7]

```
def make_smallnet():
  SIZE = 224
  model = Sequential()
  model.add(Conv2D(32, (3, 3), activation="relu",
  input_shape=(SIZE, SIZE, 3)))
  model.add(MaxPooling2D((2, 2)))
```

```
model.add(Conv2D(32, (3, 3), activation="relu"))
model.add(MaxPooling2D((2, 2)))
model.add(Conv2D(32, (3, 3), activation="relu"))

model.add(Flatten())
model.add(Dense(32, activation="relu"))
model.add(Dense(1, activation="sigmoid"))

model.compile(optimizer=Adam(learning_rate=1e-2),
              loss='binary_crossentropy',
              metrics=['accuracy', Recall(name='recall'),
                  Precision(name='precision'),
                  AUC(name='auc')])

return model
```

This method will be used to return a "compiled" model in our final training method (note: a "compiled" model is just a model that is ready to be trained). This network architecture contains multiple layers ordered in a sequential manner (i.e., each layer feeds into next one directly); we call this a sequential convolutional neural network. This convolutional neural network (CNN) is split up into two main components: a convolutional part and a dense part.

In the convolutional part (before the line that says "Flatten()"), we create three convolutional layers and two max pooling layers. The first convolutional layer is specified with the Conv2D method from the Keras neural network library.

Let's break down this statement a bit further:

```
Conv2D(32, (3, 3), activation="relu", input_shape=(SIZE, SIZE, 3))
```

The first argument 32 specifies the number of convolutional filters we want to train. Recall that these filters slide over an image from left to right and multiply the pixels that the filter is on by whatever values are learned in the filter. We're doing this process 32 times.

185

The filter size is specified by the second argument (3,3), meaning that a 3px x 3px square is going to be moving around our image and doing multiplication.

The `activation="relu"` argument specifies the activation function of the convolutional layer. This is basically a function that is applied to the resulting values coming out of the image convolutions. In this case, we use the "relu" activation function which will keep positive values and set any negative values to 0. We need activation functions since that is what allows the network to do gradient descent (i.e., figure out what's the best way to adjust weights to minimize loss).

The last argument specifies what the input shape is for the image. Here, we have it set to (SIZE, SIZE, 3). From the method body, SIZE is a variable we set equal to 224, which corresponds to the size of the input images we get from our training generator. The "3" represents the fact that our image is an RGB color image. Even though x-ray radiographs just have intensity values and no color, the Kaggle contest organizers saved the x-ray DICOM images to a .jpg format, which converts them to RGB color images (even though they appear as gray to our eyes). The "3" represents that there are actually three images stacked upon each other for each image: one image containing the "red" values for the image, another containing the "green" values, and the last containing the "blue" values. If we had raw intensity values, we would have changed the "3" out for a "1." We wrap this Conv2D method call in a `model.add` which will actually add this convolutional layer (created by Conv2D) to the sequential CNN model we're making.

> **Side Note**: When we're actually training this layer of the network, the neural network will need to learn several hundred parameters just for this layer alone. The specific number of parameters (think of these as the weights and biases of the perceptrons, though there aren't any in the convolutional filters)

is 896. How do we calculate that number? Well, each of the filters is 3x3x3 (the first two "3s" indicate the width and height of the filter; the last 3 represents the fact that we're operating on a three-channeled color image) in size where each unit of the filter is a parameter to learn. Additionally, there is a general "bias" term that must be learned for each filter as well. We have 32 of these filters to learn, meaning that there are $32 * ((3 * 3 * 3) + 1) = 896$ parameters to learn. If we have outputs from the prior layer, we'll also need to learn parameters to determine their weight. The general formula for the parameters to learn in a convolution block is

$$\#\,parameters = \#\,filters * \left(\left(\frac{\text{filter height} * \text{filter width} * \#\,\text{of filters in}}{\text{previous layer}} \right) + 1 \right)$$

The second layer we're adding to our network is a "max pooling layer" (a.k.a. maxpool). All this layer will do is downsize our image by looking in specific blocks of our picture and only keeping the highest-valued pixels. In this case, since we pass the numbers (2,2) to the MaxPool2D layer, we are going to break up the image output from the previous convolutional layer into little 2x2 sections (nonoverlapping). This layer will then pick out the highest-valued pixel within each of the 2x2 sections. There aren't any parameters to learn since this operation is just an algorithmic step to downsize our input.

We'll repeat the convolution ➤ maxpool operations in order once again and follow up with a last convolution layer. Adding more convolutions to our network can produce potentially better results; however, we need to make sure that we don't add too many maxpool layers, since each time they are applied, the image is downsized by two. Speaking of, what is the size of our image at the end of these operations?

After the first Conv2D operation, our input 224 x 244 image will be converted to a 222 x 222 x 32 image. Why did we lose two pixels on either side and add an "x32"? Well, the convolution filters that pass over the image must always pass over valid parts of the image (i.e., we can't have a situation where some parts of the filter are on the image and some parts are off the image). Additionally, since we have 32 convolutional filters, we're essentially creating 32 new images for a single input image. This leads us to the following general formula for how to calculate dimension changes in convolutions:

$$dnew = \left[(d - k + 2p) / s \right] + 1$$

Here, d is the size of the original dimension we want to find the new dimension size for (e.g., width), k is the size of the kernel along the same dimension, p is the padding parameter, and s is the stride parameter. The output of the formula is the $dnew$ dimension size. Let's try calculating our new width. Since our width input dimension size is 224, d is 224. k is the width of our filter which is 3. Padding (p, the number of pixels we add to the edges of our image) is 0 (this is default unless otherwise specified). Stride (s, how much the filter moves over on each step) is just 1. Plugging it in, $[(224-3+2*0)/1)]+1 = 222$. Since our input height is the same as the input width and the filter height is the same as the filter width, our new height is 222. The x32 comes from the fact that there are 32 filters, each creating a new image.

After the max pool operation, our dimensions will go down by half. In the case that our original dimensions are odd numbered, we round down. So that means that our new dimensions after the maxpool layer would be 111 (222/2) for the width and height and 32 for the channels (a.k.a. number of images that were produced from a convolution).

The next convolution layer is the same as the first, but this time we increase the number of channels from 32 to 64. Running through the math, the new width and height dimensions will be $[(111-3+2*0)/1]+1 = 109$.

The new number of channels will be 64, producing a final dimension of 111 x 111 x 64. We then follow that up with a maxpool, which brings dimensions down to 111/2 = 54.5 (round down) = 54 (final size = 54 x 54 x 64). Next, we have another convolution operation that keeps the number of channels the same, so the final dimensions are 52 x 52 x 64. As you can see, each maxpool operation can reduce our image size and we can't go below a 1x1 image (also note that convolutions can downsize an image if the stride is > 1).

The total number of parameters to learn for the second convolution is 18496 (64 $*$ ((3 $*$ 3 $*$ 32) + 1), and the number of parameters in the third convolution is 36928 (64 $*$ ((3 $*$ 3 $*$ 64) + 1)). As you can see, we already have over 56,000 parameters to learn, and we aren't even done specifying our network.

The next block of code will take the convolved images we have (a 64-channel image with dimensions 52 x 52) and "flatten" it so that they now represent individual perceptrons. In fact, we create 173,056 ($ = 52*52*64$) perceptrons in total. This is done just with the call to model.add(Flatten()).

Next, we densely connect the 173,056 perceptrons to 64 perceptrons (by specifying model.add(Dense(64...))). This connects each of the 173,056 perceptrons to each of the 64 perceptrons, forming a total of 173065*64 connections (these are parameters we need to learn). Additionally, we'll need to learn a bias for each of the 64 perceptrons, so that brings the total number of parameters to learn for this layer up to 11075648. We also set a relu activation function on this layer (sets negative outputs to 0, doesn't alter positive outputs). This leads us to the final line of code for this dense layer model.add(Dense(64, activation="relu")). Note, all of the aforementioned layers, Conv2D, MaxPool2D, Flatten, and Dense, come from the tensorflow.keras.layers submodule (which contains many, many other layers for you to check out).

Finally, we have the last layer of our network. This is the only one that is actually constrained to be a specific value since the output of this layer is what we'll be using to evaluate a prediction. We will set up a dense layer but only have one output perceptron. That means that all the 64 perceptrons from the previous layer will be connected to this one output layer (and we need to learn 64 weights + 1 bias parameter = 65 parameters for this layer). We'll also set a "sigmoid" activation function on this layer (constrains outputs from 0 to 1 along an "S" curve; refer to Figure 6-3 for comparison between sigmoid and relu functions). Graphs of these activation functions can be found in Figure 6-3.

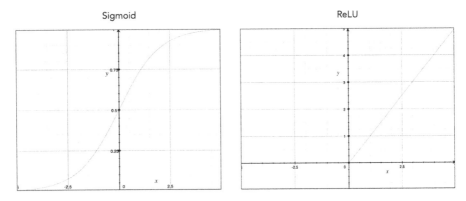

Figure 6-3. *Sigmoid and ReLU activation function graphs*

> **Side Note**: Consider the preactivation function
> output of a neuron as the "x" value fed into these
> functions. In the sigmoid function, no matter what
> x value we put in, the y value will always be in the
> range of 0 to 1. In the relu function, if we input a
> positive x value, we get a positive y value out. If
> x is negative, we get 0 out. There are many other
> activation functions out there such as identity,
> binary step, logistic, tanh, arctan, leaky relu,
> softplus, and more.

But why do we choose our output to just be a single perceptron that has a sigmoid function attached to it? Our classification task is a binary classification, meaning that there are only two possible outputs. Really, this can be represented with a single value in the range of 0 to 1; hence, we only need one output to represent it. If the output value is below some threshold (such as 0.5), we'll consider the output to be normal; otherwise, it would be a pneumonia. A perfect prediction would yield an output value of either 1 or 0 (pneumonia or normal); however, that rarely happens. But the raw output value from the perceptron can also be considered a probability that something is considered to be a pneumonia case (since the output is constrained between 0 and 1), which is useful to give a "confidence" that the image is pneumonia. In the case that you adapt this network for some other task, you should set the number of dense outputs to the number of distinct categories you have if the number of categories is > 2.

The last segment of code consists of the model compilation statement. This statement contains information about what is the loss function of the model (`loss='binary_crossentropy'`), what is the optimizer used to dictate its learning rate (`optimizer='adam'`), and what metrics should be reported on each training step (the list starting with `metrics=['accuracy', ...]`).

The loss function is set to `binary_crossentropy`. Recall that a loss function is used to quantify how wrong the neural network is and, more importantly, is a critical component in determining how the neural network adjusts its weights and biases in the backpropagation process. The binary cross entropy formula is as follows:

$$-\frac{1}{N}\sum_{i=1}^{N} y_i \log\big(p(y_i)\big) + (1 - y_i)\log\big(1 - p(y_i)\big)$$

This looks complicated, but what does it actually do? Let's say that the neural network last perceptron outputs 0.73 for some sample. This sample is actually a pneumonia sample, so if our network was the best it could possibly be, it should be outputting a 1. Clearly the network needs to improve to get to that point, and accordingly, it should be told how "wrong" it is. We can do that using the binary cross entropy formula. Ignoring the summation term for the moment, let $p(y_i)$ equal 0.73 and let y_i equal 1. Also, we're going to use a log base 2 rather than base 10. The loss is going to be $1*\log(0.73)+(1-1)\log(1-0.73)=-0.31$. Note, we need to flip the sign since loss is typically referred to as a positive number that should be minimized, so the final loss is 0.31. Let's try out another example. Let's say that the last perceptron outputs a value of 0.73 but for that an image that is truly normal. This is *really* bad since the network should ideally output a "0" in this case. Let's see what the loss would be: $0*\log(0.73)+(1-0)*\log(1-0.73)=-1.309$. Flipping the sign, we get a final loss of 1.309.

We just saw how having a close prediction yielded a lower loss compared to a really far off prediction. This is the exact behavior we want since our neural network aims to always decrease the output of the loss function for each batch. For all the images in a batch (taken care of by the $\sum_{i=1}^{N}$ term), we simply sum up their losses and takes its average and multiply it by -1 (taken care of by the $-\frac{1}{N}$). If you were going to predict multiple categories, you'd use a "categorical cross entropy" loss function which is very similar to the loss function described earlier. For regression tasks (e.g., predicting degree of spinal curvature from a radiograph), you could use a mean squared error loss (difference between predicted and actual value squared).

Now let's move on to the optimizer. The optimizer we're using is called "Adam" which is short for adaptive moment estimation. For each of the parameters in our model, it will change the learning rate (i.e., how much the weights or biases associated with the parameter will change) based on whether the parameter is associated with frequent features (in which case it will keep learning rates low) or infrequent features (in which case it will keep learning rates high). There is a lot more nuance into what makes the "Adam" optimizer work and how it is different from some other optimizers such as stochastic gradient descent, adagrad, rmsprop, etc.; however, it isn't worth going into (but if you want to look at it, here is all the math behind those). In general, it is popularly used, and, more importantly, it is readily available in the Keras library so that we only need to specify a single line that says `optimizer='adam'` when we compile the model.

Lastly, we specify metrics we want to keep track of at ever training step and then return the model from the method. The metrics are specified in a list argument to the compile method and are as follows: 'accuracy' (which is recognizable by Keras with just the string itself), recall, precision, and AUC. The names are self-explanatory and will just print out the accuracy, recall, precision, and area under the curve (for the ROC curve) at each training step in the model. For the last three metrics, we can specify a "name" parameter that dictates how they show up during the training process as the model metrics are printed out. Also note that the last three metrics are all coming from a Keras submodule called `tensorflow.keras.metrics`.

Now that we've set up smallnet, we're just one step away from training the network. Before we do that, we need to set up some callbacks which will allow us to monitor the progress of the network, save its best training cycle, stop it if it doesn't improve, and kick it out of any learning rate plateaus.

Callbacks: TensorBoard, Early Stopping, Model Checkpointing, and Reduce Learning Rates

We're going to define a method called `get_callbacks` that returns a list of callbacks for use later in the training process. Let's see what that method looks like:

INPUT[CELL=8]

```
def get_callbacks(model_name):

    logdir = (
        f'logs/scalars/{model_name}_{datetime.now().
        strftime("%m%d%Y-%H%M%S")}'
    )
```

```
tb = TensorBoard(log_dir=logdir)
es = EarlyStopping(
        monitor="val_loss",
        min_delta=1,
        patience=20,
        verbose=2,
        mode="min",
        restore_best_weights=True,
    )
mc = ModelCheckpoint(f'model_{model_name}.hdf5',
                        save_best_only=True,
                        verbose=0,
                        monitor='val_loss',
                        mode='min')

rlr = ReduceLROnPlateau(monitor='val_loss',
                        factor=0.3,
                        patience=3,
                        min_lr=0.000001,
                        verbose=1)
return [tb, es, mc, rlr]
```

The get_callbacks method just takes in a single argument called model_name, and this is just the name of the model which will help us while saving some files related to the model (to ensure that it doesn't overwrite anything else that exists on our file system).

The first callback we're going to use is the TensorBoard callback. TensorBoard is a visualization tool which we'll see later on. But it basically allows us to see how the training process went by giving us the ability to monitor the various metrics we defined. Figure 6-4 shows what TensorBoard looks like.

Figure 6-4. *TensorBoard visualization*

And it can be loaded either before or after you start your training process by running the following cell (but we won't do that until we're done training everything):

```
%load_ext tensorboard
%tensorboard --logdir logs
```

If you notice, at the top right, we're viewing the scalars panel which is the set of all the different metrics we have. TensorBoard will automatically read from a directory (specified by `--logdir FOLDERNAME`, in this case `logs`) and try to find TensorBoard log files. Those TensorBoard log files are only generated if you pass the TensorBoard callback to your neural network when you set it up for training; otherwise, it doesn't have anything to plot. Those log files will contain all of the metrics (a.k.a. scalars) at every

195

time point along the training and validation process. TensorBoard will then plot those curves for you to view (which can be helpful to determine if your network is actually still improving or not).

All we need to specify for the TensorBoard callback is the file path of the directory where the logs should be kept. Since we may be running our network multiple times, we want to make sure that previous runs aren't overwritten. We can do this by including the date and time the network was run in the folder path. The `datetime` library provides a submodule called `datetime` that has a `.now()` method on it which allows us to get the current time as a Python object. We can convert it to a string by calling `.strftime()` on `datetime.now()` and passing in the following string `"%m%d%Y-%H%M%S"` which is shorthand for printing the month (%m), day (%d), and year (%Y), followed by a "-" sign and then the current hour (%H, 24-hour time), minute (%M), and second (%S). If I run this on July 26 at 12:24 PM and 36 seconds, the resulting string would be 07272021-122436. We interpolate this value into the general string `"logs/scalars/{model_name}_{the date + time}"`.

The second callback is the EarlyStopping callback. As the name may imply, it will stop the training of the network early (meaning that if we set our network to train 100 epochs, this callback could stop its training at the end of some epoch number if certain conditions are met). Why would we want to do that? It is very useful to prevent overfitting for our model. If we monitor the validation loss and don't see it improves by 1% over 20 epochs, that likely means that the network is done learning all it can. `monitor="val_loss"` tells the callback to keep an eye on the validation loss. `min_delta=1` tells the callback to see if it has improved by 1% (in the downward direction as dictated by `mode='min'`) after `patience=20` epochs. `verbose=2` is used to print out when it stops the network early. Lastly, we will set the model back to the best point (specified by `restore_best_weights=True`).

The third callback is the `ModelCheckpoint` callback. This callback will save a version of the model to Colab's file system every epoch (with some caveats). The first argument is just what the name of the model filename should be (in this case it would be `'model_smallnet.hdf5'` since `model_name` will be "smallnet") (stay tuned for where we pass this argument in). However, we've also specified a `save_best_only=True` argument, meaning that we will only save the model at the end of each epoch if it beat out the previously saved model. How do we determine what model won? We look at the validation loss (specified in the argument `monitor='val_loss'`) and will pick whichever is lower (`mode='min'`). After we're done training the model, we could download the model_smallnet.hdf5 file and re-upload it to Colab/run it on our local machine if we want to.

The last callback is the `ReduceLROnPlateau` callback. In general, a learning rate that is too high will result in the network failing to converge. In most cases, the Adam optimizer should be able to adjust the learning rate on its own, but sometimes, it will need some forced decrease in the baseline learning rate to continue optimizing further and getting the network to continue learning. It will reduce the learning rate by a factor of 0.3 (`factor=0.3`) if the validation loss has not changed for 3 epochs (`monitor='val_loss'`, `patience=3`) and will continue to do so until the learning rate is 0.000001 (`min_lr=0.000001`). It will also print when it lowers the learning rate (`verbose=1`).

Now that we've defined all our callbacks, let's get started with defining how the training happens!

Defining the Fit Method and Fitting Smallnet

We're going to make a single method that calls the make smallnet method and the get callbacks method while also training the network. We'll also see how we can get a summary of the model (i.e., all the layers it has) and a plot of how all the model layers feed into each other. Here's the definition for that method. **NOTE**: We will be coming back to this method later, so you'll need to edit it in a couple of sections (I'm denoting that it is a work in progress by noting a WIP tag next to the cell number).

INPUT[CELL=9][WIP v1]

```
def fit_model(train_generator, validation_generator,
model_name,
              batch_size=32, epochs=15):

  if model_name == 'smallnet':
    model = make_smallnet()

  model.summary()

  plot_model(model, to_file=model_name + '.jpg',
  show_shapes=True)

  model_history = model.fit(train_generator,
                            validation_data=validation_
                            generator,
                            steps_per_epoch=train_
                            generator.n/batch_size,
                            validation_steps=validation_
                            generator.n/batch_size,
                            epochs=epochs,
                            verbose=1,
                            callbacks=get_callbacks(model_
                            name))
  return model, model_history
```

All this method does is the following:

1. It takes in the train and validation generators we
    made earlier. These will be used during the model
    fitting process (data will be trained on the training
    generator images; it will be evaluated at each epoch
    on the validation generator images).

2. It checks to see if the model_name we pass in is
    equal to 'smallnet'. If it is, we will call the make_
    smallnet() method which returns a compiled Keras
    model to us (which we will store in model).

3. We will then print out a model summary (using
    model.summary()) which contains information
    about the number of layers, sizes of each layer, and
    number of parameters to be trained.

4. Then we'll call a method plot_model (defined in the
    tensorflow.keras.utils submodule) and pass in
    our model, the filename we'd like to save the plot_
    model results to (just the model name appended
    with a .jpg to indicate it is an image file) and the
    show_shapes=True argument (which makes the
    diagram a bit fancier). This will produce that shown
    in Figure 6-5 of our model once we call it (this will
    be in the Colab files directory; refresh it if you don't
    see it).

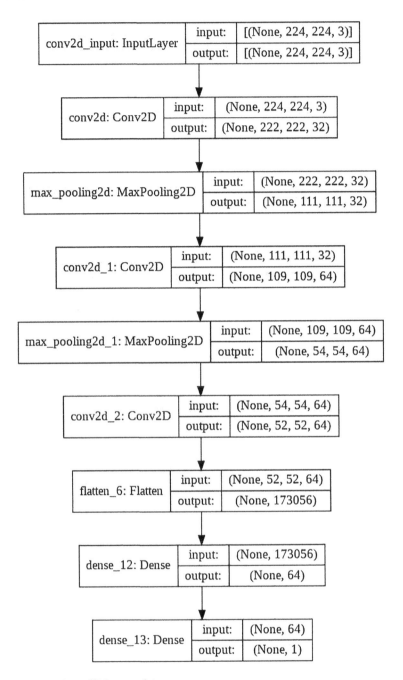

Figure 6-5. *SmallNet architecture output*

Notice how it has all of the layers we specified: the three convolutional layers, the two max pooling layers, the flatten layer, and the two dense layers. It also has an input layer that is added by Keras to represent the image input.

Lastly, we call model.fit which actually trains our model. It takes in the training generator and the validation generator (validation_ data=validation_generator) and also requires information about the number of steps we need for training and validation. A step is considered to be one run through a batch of images, so all the steps would be the number of batches. We can get that just by calling generator_name.n (gets us the total number of images) and dividing it by batch_size (a default named argument in the method declaration). steps_per_epoch is equal to the number of batches in the training generator, and validations_steps is equal to the number of batches in the validation generator. We set verbose=1 to get progress notes on training and set the callbacks to the result of the get_callbacks() method call (which just returns a list of the callbacks we wanted to keep track of).

The model.fit call returns the history of the model (which is just what the metrics were at each epoch for the training and validation sets). At the end of the method, we return the trained model (in model) and its history model_history.

Now that we've specified the method to train the SmallNet network, let's actually train it. Note: running the next cell will take approximately 30 minutes.

INPUT[CELL=10]

```
small_model, small_model_hist = fit_model(train_generator,
                                          validation_generator,
                                          'smallnet', epochs=15)
```

OUTPUT
Refer to Figure 6-6.

```
small_model, small_model_hist = fit_model(train_generator, validation_generator, 'smallnet', epochs=15)

Model: "sequential"
_____
Layer (type)                 Output Shape              Param #
=================================================================
conv2d (Conv2D)              (None, 222, 222, 32)      896
_____
max_pooling2d (MaxPooling2D) (None, 111, 111, 32)      0
_____
conv2d_1 (Conv2D)            (None, 109, 109, 64)      18496
_____
max_pooling2d_1 (MaxPooling2 (None, 54, 54, 64)        0
_____
conv2d_2 (Conv2D)            (None, 52, 52, 64)        36928
_____
flatten_6 (Flatten)          (None, 173056)            0
_____
dense_12 (Dense)             (None, 64)                11075648
_____
dense_13 (Dense)             (None, 1)                 65
=================================================================
Total params: 11,132,033
Trainable params: 11,132,033
Non-trainable params: 0
_____
Epoch 1/15
117/117 [==============================] - 95s 798ms/step - loss: 0.5629 - accuracy: 0.7769 - recall: 0.9218 - precision: 0.8032 - auc: 0.7754
Epoch 2/15
117/117 [==============================] - 93s 793ms/step - loss: 0.2553 - accuracy: 0.8887 - recall: 0.9302 - precision: 0.9191 - auc: 0.9481
Epoch 3/15
117/117 [==============================] - 92s 786ms/step - loss: 0.2275 - accuracy: 0.9125 - recall: 0.9418 - precision: 0.9391 - auc: 0.9592
Epoch 4/15
117/117 [==============================] - 92s 789ms/step - loss: 0.2060 - accuracy: 0.9168 - recall: 0.9425 - precision: 0.9439 - auc: 0.9666
Epoch 5/15
117/117 [==============================] - 91s 780ms/step - loss: 0.2011 - accuracy: 0.9178 - recall: 0.9436 - precision: 0.9443 - auc: 0.9677

Epoch 00005: ReduceLROnPlateau reducing learning rate to 0.0003000000142492354.
Epoch 6/15
117/117 [==============================] - 90s 770ms/step - loss: 0.1674 - accuracy: 0.9370 - recall: 0.9553 - precision: 0.9587 - auc: 0.9767
Epoch 7/15
117/117 [==============================] - 91s 779ms/step - loss: 0.1659 - accuracy: 0.9328 - recall: 0.9498 - precision: 0.9582 - auc: 0.9776
Epoch 8/15
```

Figure 6-6. *Output during model training*

In this output, we can see some interesting things. For one thing, in the first part (before the "epoch"), we get the model summary (generated from `model.summary()`). It looks like our calculation for the number of parameters and dimensions per layer from earlier was correct! This model summary is useful to help you determine if you're on the right track and have specified your model correctly.

After you see that, you'll see the training process begin. We specified that we should train our network for 15 epochs. Within each epoch, there are 117 steps which represent the 117 training batches we have. After each step, you'll see the "loss" and other metrics update: these are the training metrics the network reports after it sees all the images in each step (i.e., one batch). At each epoch (i.e., a run through all 117 training batches), you'll see that the `loss` printed out will start to decrease over time. Here, we saw it go from 0.56 to 0.25 to 0.1659 in jury 7 epochs. We also see the training set accuracy (`accuracy` in the printed text) go from 77.69% to 93.28%. You can also see all of the other metrics we specified: recall, precision, and AUC. If you scroll your output to the right after an epoch is finished training, you'll also see those same metrics on the validation set (those metrics are prepended with the val_ string). If you see these validation metrics deviate far from the training metrics, that's a sign that you're overfitting your network.

You'll also see in the previous output that at epoch 5, we reduced our learning rate to 0.0003 since the ReduceLRonPlateau callback condition was triggered. This was because the validation loss val_loss was plateauing (it went from 0.43 to 0.20 to 0.24 to 0.21 to 0.25) rather than constantly decreasing. This happened again at epoch 14 for me, but it might not happen for you. After the decrease in learning rate, the val_loss started decreasing again, and I also saw that val_accuracy increased quickly.

We can even view the training session by starting up a TensorBoard with the following:

INPUT[CELL=optional but after 10]

```
%load_ext tensorboard
%tensorboard --logdir logs
```

At the end of the training session, metrics were as follows:

- **Validation Accuracy**: 0.9402

- **Validation Recall**: 0.9608

- **Validation Precision**: 0.9580

- **Validation AUC**: 0.9794

These are excellent statistics on a network we defined on our own! Before we get to evaluating the performance of this model, let's go ahead and define another model that could potentially beat out our 94% accuracy.

Your Second Convolutional Neural Network: Transfer Learning with VGG16

SmallNet was great for this task; however, there are other neural network architectures that are tried and tested rather than the relatively simple toy one we just made. One of these architectures is called VGG16. Admittedly, it is a bit old by deep learning standards (it was made back in 2014); however, it blew its competition out of the water on the ImageNet classification challenge (learn how to classify 14 million images into 1000 classes). VGG16 contains 13 convolutional layers and 3 dense layers, netting a total of over 14 million parameters to train. Since it did so well on the ImageNet contest, it is likely that the weights and biases "learned" how to extract salient image features that were generalizable to the 1000 different classes it was originally trained to classify images into. As a result, it may be useful for us to somehow leverage the existing weights and biases to make our classification task better since VGG16 seems to have done such a good job recognizing images in general.

However, the issue is that we can't use VGG16 directly. Unfortunately, the ImageNet challenge didn't contain any training images using x-rays and definitely didn't have a class for pneumonia vs. normal. But maybe there's some way to keep the main convolutional part of the network and just remove the last layer of the network which (as we covered in the smallnet discussion) was where we get the classification values from. Just as SmallNet has a last-layer perceptron for each class (just 1 in this case), so too does VGG16 have a last-layer set of perceptrons (exactly 1000) for classifying ImageNet images. If we just rip out the last dense layer with 1000 perceptrons from the VGG16 model that was trained on the ImageNet challenge, we could leverage the convolutional weights that were internal to the network (i.e., the weights that were really good at extracting image features to learn on). This process of using weights from a previously trained network for a new purpose is known as "transfer learning."

> **Side Note**: Another possibility would be to just take
> the VGG16 architecture and train it from scratch.
> Unfortunately, it takes a long time to converge to a
> point where it accurately predicts data and is better
> suited to be trained on much larger datasets. As
> we'll shortly demonstrate, it is actually sufficient to
> train the network on the preexisting weights to get a
> very good accuracy.

Let's see how to do that. After the cell where you defined the make_
smallnet() method (cell 7), insert the following make_VGGnet method:

INPUT[CELL=New Cell after Cell #7]

```
def make_VGGnet():
  SIZE = 224
  m = VGG16(weights = 'imagenet',
                include_top = False,
                input_shape = (SIZE, SIZE, 3))
  for layer in m.layers:
    layer.trainable = False

  x = Flatten()(m.output)
  x = Dense(4096, activation="relu")(x)
  x = Dense(1072, activation="relu")(x)
  x = Dropout(0.2)(x)
  predictions = Dense(1, activation="sigmoid")(x)

  model = Model(inputs=m.input, outputs=predictions)
  ## Compile and run

  adam = Adam(learning_rate=0.001)
  model.compile(optimizer=adam,
                loss='binary_crossentropy',
                metrics=['accuracy', Recall(name='recall'),
```

```
                          Precision(name='precision'),
                          AUC(name='auc')])
return model
```

Going line by line

- We define the size of the input image we're going to
  accept in the variable SIZE which will be passed into
  other methods. We'll keep it at 224 since that is the
  default input size for the VGG16 model.

- We then instantiate a new VGG16 model object
  by calling VGG16. We specify that we want to
  use the weights from the ImageNet dataset
  (weights='imagenet'), we don't want to include the
  last layer of the network that was used to make the 1000
  classifications (include_top=False), and we want to
  input 224 x 224 x 3 images (input_shape = (SIZE,
  SIZE, 3), note the 3 represents the fact that the image
  has 3 color channels). We store this network instance in
  the variable m.

- Then we loop through all the layers in the network (for
  layer in m.layers) and set the trainable property
  on each layer to False. This will stop the weights
  learned in the ImageNet competition from being
  altered (a.k.a. "freezing" the weights), which is exactly
  what we want since we need to preserve the ability
  of VGG16 to extract image features like it did in the
  ImageNet dataset.

- We then define some additional layers to add to
  the network. Note, when we made smallnet, we did
  this with model.add. In this case, I want to show

you a different way to do it that you may see more
often online:

- First, we'll flatten the output layer of the altered VGG16
  model we have stored in m by calling Flatten()(m.
  output). This syntax may seem weird, but what Flatten
  is doing is actually returning a method that accepts a
  single input, the output of the prior layer to append
  this flatten layer to. We assign the updated model to the
  variable x.

- Then, we'll create a densely connected layer with 4096
  perceptrons that has a relu activation function attached
  to it, passing in x to continue adding that layer to the
  model (Dense(4096, activation="relu")(x)). We'll
  assign this value back to x.

- Similarly, we'll make another densely connected layer
  with 1072 perceptrons.

- We'll add in a "Dropout" layer which will randomly
  zero out 20% (Dropout(0.2)) of the input weights
  from the previous layer to the next layer randomly at
  each step in the training process. This helps prevent
  overfitting since some weights are left out of some
  parts of the training process (since their weight is set
  to 0 by the dropout layer) each time a training step is
  completed.

- Then, we'll add in the single perceptron dense layer
  that is similar to what we had as our last layer for
  SmallNet. We assign this to the variable predictions.

- Lastly (before compiling the model), we need to tell
  Keras that this is a normal model by instantiating a

> plain Model object with the input size (inputs=m.
> input) and the outputs (which contain all of the
> prior layers). Currently, we have the layers stored in
> predictions, so we pass it to the outputs= named
> parameter.

To compile our network, we need to use a non-default version of the Adam optimizer (just to show you how you could specify parameters on optimizers that aren't necessarily the default). We use the Adam optimizer from tensorflow.keras.optimizers and set its initial learning rate to 0.001, resulting in the final line adam = Adam(learning_rate=0.001). We pass in the same loss and metrics to this model.compile method as we did for SmallNet and return the model from this method.

To run this method, we'll need to change our fit_model method a little bit, and, while we're at it, let's also give ourselves the ability to take a trained version of a model we generated and continue training it:

INPUT[CELL=9][FINAL]

```
def fit_model(train_generator, validation_generator,
model_name,
                 batch_size=32, epochs=15, model_fname=None):
  if model_fname == None:
    if model_name == 'smallnet':
      model = make_smallnet()
    if model_name == 'vgg':
      model = make_VGGnet()
    model.summary()
    plot_model(model, to_file=model_name + '.jpg',
    show_shapes=True)
  else:
    model = load_model(model_fname)

  ...# REST IS THE SAME!
```

208

```
model_history = model.fit(train_generator,
                          validation_data=validation_
                          generator,
                          steps_per_epoch=train_
                          generator.n/batch_size,
                          validation_steps=validation_
                          generator.n/batch_size,
                          epochs=epochs,
                          verbose=1,
                          callbacks=get_callbacks(model_
                          name))
    return model, model_history
```

First off, we've specified a new method argument called model_fname. This argument will take in the string file path to a trained model. If it isn't specified, its default value is none, and we go into the first part of the if else branch at the beginning of the method. In here, we've added another if statement to check to see if the model_name is 'vgg' (if it is, we call the make VGG method we just made).

If we do happen to have a model we've trained that we want to train further, we can do that by specifying an argument to model_fname. Recall that we generated a pretrained model with the filename model_ INSERTMODELNAME.hdf5 each time our ModelCheckpoint callback triggers (i.e., whenever we have a "best" epoch). If you check in your Colab notebook file pane, you should see that you have a model_smallnet.hdf5.

Now that we've actually set up our vgg net to be called from the fit_ model method we just edited, let's call it

INPUT[CELL=11]

```
vgg_model, vgg_model_hist = fit_model(train_generator,
                                      validation_generator,
                                      'vgg', epochs=15)
```

OUTPUT

Model: "model_2"

Layer (type)	Output Shape	Param #
input_6 (InputLayer)	[(None, 224, 224, 3)]	0
block1_conv1 (Conv2D)	(None, 224, 224, 64)	1792
block1_conv2 (Conv2D)	(None, 224, 224, 64)	36928
block1_pool (MaxPooling2D)	(None, 112, 112, 64)	0

```
...LOTS OF OTHER LAYERS THAT ARE OMITTED....
=================================================================
Total params: 121,872,289
Trainable params: 107,157,601
Non-trainable params: 14,714,688
```

```
...EPOCHS ALSO OMITTED
```

Wow, we have over 107 million parameters to train. The non-trainable params are the weights that we froze when we called `layer.trainable = False` on each of the original VGG16 layers. The remaining 107,157,601 parameters are the ones we defined in our dense layers (a couple of dense layers add several million parameters very quickly!).

If we look at the training progress, we see that it tends to go a little bit more smoothly (only trips the ReduceLRonPlateau callback once), and we generally see higher accuracies and AUCs which is great! I got a final validation accuracy of 96.58% which is an improvement from 93.28%.

Let's compare how the training process went for both of these networks before we dive a bit deeper into evaluation metrics.

In case you aren't able to use TensorBoard (it is sometimes buggy), you can plot out the history for training vs. validation accuracy and loss for both networks using the following method:

INPUT[CELL=12]

```python
def plot_history(history):

    fig = plt.figure(figsize = (18 , 6))

    fig.add_subplot(1,2,1)
    plt.plot(history.history['loss'])
    plt.plot(history.history['val_loss'])
    plt.title('model loss')
    plt.xlabel('epoch')
    plt.ylabel('loss')
    plt.legend(['train loss', 'valid loss'])
    plt.grid(True)
    plt.plot()

    fig.add_subplot(1,2,2)
    plt.plot(history.history['accuracy'])
    plt.plot(history.history['val_accuracy'])
    plt.title('model accuracy')
    plt.xlabel('epoch')
    plt.ylabel('accuracy')
    plt.legend(['train acc', 'valid acc'])
    plt.grid(True)
    plt.plot()
```

All we do here is define a method called plot history which takes in a model training history which we get as one of the values returned from model.fit and (in turn) fit_model(). We create a figure and add a subplot (there will be two images, arranged in one row with two columns). The first image will plot the history.history['loss'] and history.

history['val_loss'] arrays which are the training and validation loss at the end of every epoch. We title that plot "model loss" and set the x-axis label to "epoch" and the y label to "loss." We also give a legend for each of the lines: the first line will be called "train loss," and the second line will be called "valid loss" (matplotlib knows what legend item to match up to which line based on the order the lines were plotted with plt.plot(). Lastly, we choose to show a grid and plot that data. We repeat the same process for another graph but do it for training accuracy and validation accuracy. Let's see what the result is after calling it:

INPUT[CELL=13]

plot_history(small_model_hist)

OUTPUT

Refer to Figure 6-7 for a plot of model history for SmallNet.

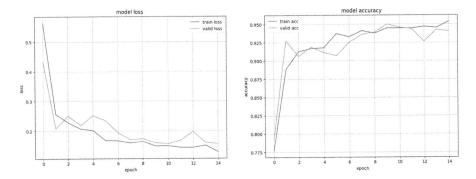

Figure 6-7. *SmallNet model history*

INPUT[CELL=14]

plot_history(vgg_model_hist)

OUTPUT

Refer to Figure 6-8 for a plot of model history for VGG16.

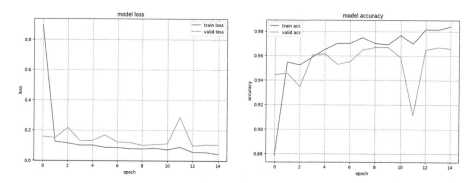

Figure 6-8. *VGG16 model training history*

We can see that the VGG network actually seems to have had a difficult time around epoch 11. This probably coincided with the reduction in the learning rate. However, we can see that the validation and accuracy curves follow each other relatively closely, indicating that we aren't overfitting so far.

Now that we've viewed the training curves, let's take a look at what the network actually pays attention to when it evaluates the images with a technique called Grad-CAM.

Visualizing Outputs with Grad-CAM

Grad-CAM is an algorithm that allows us to generate heatmaps that show which parts of the image contributed most to the network's ultimate classification decision. It is possible to get a great deal of intuition based on the Grad-CAM images and seeing how they work. Without further ado, let's get started.

We'll be using a library called VizGradCam. Unfortunately, it isn't available on the pip package management system, so we'll need to download it directly from the author's GitHub page (this is a website that hosts code that anyone can view, a.k.a. open source code). We'll do that with the following block:

INPUT[CELL=13]

```
!git clone https://github.com/gkeechin/vizgradcam.git
!cp vizgradcam/gradcam.py gradcam.py
```

OUTPUT

```
Cloning into 'vizgradcam'...
remote: Enumerating objects: 64, done.
remote: Counting objects: 100% (64/64), done.
remote: Compressing objects: 100% (57/57), done.
remote: Total 64 (delta 30), reused 24 (delta 7), pack-reused 0
Unpacking objects: 100% (64/64), done.
```

If you see that, you're all set. We've downloaded the VizGradCam code and have taken out the file that contains the functionality we need and copied it to our main directory.

Next, we'll define a method that allows us to get Grad-CAM outputs and also prints out our predictions + their confidence.

INPUT[CELL=14]

```
from gradcam import VizGradCAM

def display_map_and_conf(model, test_generator):
  imgs = test_generator.next()
  fig = plt.figure(figsize=(15,5))

  for i in range(3):
    fig.add_subplot(1,3,i+1)
    image = imgs[0][i]
    label = 'PNEUMONIA' if imgs[1][i] == 1 else 'NORMAL'
    VizGradCAM(model, image, plot_results=True,
    interpolant=0.5)
    out_prob = model.predict(image.reshape(1,224,224,3))[0][0]
```

```
title = f"Prediction: {'PNEUMONIA' if out_prob > 0.5 else
'NORMAL'}\n"
title += f"Prob(Pneumonia): {out_prob}\n"
title += f"True Label: {label}\n"
plt.title(title)
```

This method will take in a trained model and a test generator (we defined it earlier). It will grab one batch of images from the test generator (test_generator.next()) and then create a figure for us to plot Grad-CAM results to.

For the first three images (for i in range(3)) in our batch of images (stored in imgs), we will add a subplot to our figure (start counting at 1) and then grab the image from our batch (imgs[0][i] contains the *i*th image of the batch) and the associated label (contained in imgs[1][i]; we also recode the label to be "PNEUMONIA" if the label == 1 or "NORMAL," otherwise to aid in interpretability).

Next, we call the VizGradCam method from the library (we imported it at the top of the file using from gradcam import VizGradCAM), passing in our trained model, the image we want to visualize, and two named arguments plot_results (which plots the results to matplotlib) and interpolant (determines the relative brightness of the overlay).

Next, we get the prediction of the probability that the image is pneumonia. We do that by using a method called model.predict and passing in the image. However, our model normally expects images to be in the form of a batch, so we need to reshape the image (by calling .reshape on the image) into a 1 x 224 x 224 x 3 image (the "1" refers to the batch size). The result from the predict call is a probability in an array nested within an array, which we can get by calling model.predict(...) [0][0] (where the first [0] gets us to the first array and the second [0] gets us to the nested array).

Next, we'll make a title for the graph by string interpolating three separate strings. We append each string to each other by just adding to the variable title with a `title +=` which is the equivalent of doing `title = title + ...` (also a small side note: the \n is a special character to make a new line). For our prediction class, we define something as pneumonia if it has a probability of > 0.5; otherwise, it isn't pneumonia.

We call the method as follows:

INPUT[CELL=15]

```
display_map_and_conf(vgg_model, test_generator)
```

OUTPUT

Refer to Figure 6-9 for Grad-CAM results from VGG16.

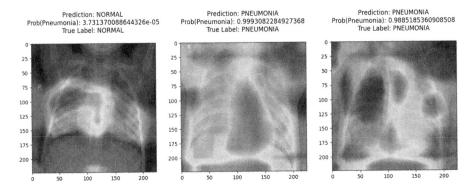

***Figure 6-9.** Grad-CAM results VGG16*

INPUT[CELL=16]

```
display_map_and_conf(small_model, test_generator)
```

OUTPUT

Refer to Figure 6-10 for Grad-CAM results from SmallNet.

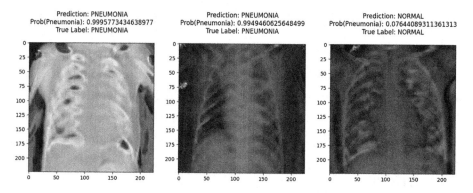

Figure 6-10. *Grad-CAM results SmallNet*

Areas in red are areas that the network paid more attention to, while areas in blue are areas that the network paid less attention to. In general, we can see that the vgg net tends to focus on anatomical structures such as the pleura in the first image. However, it also focused on the heart in the second image. And in the last image, it focused on various lobs of the lung, but also random parts of the edges. The smallnet seems to have focused on areas toward the edges in the first image, the label saying "A-P" at the upper left quadrant of the second image, and the ribs of the third image.

Overall, it seems like VGG is focusing on more anatomically relevant structures; however, it seems that it would need much more training before these heatmaps could be used to actually aid radiologists in suggesting what areas they should pay attention to. What is especially concerning however is the fact that the SmallNet focused on the A-P label in the image, possibly indicating that something about the letter labeling present in x-ray images could be hinting the network toward determining the classification rather than something about the anatomy itself. Seeing these differences is why it is important to run Grad-CAM! Now onto network evaluation.

Evaluating Performance of SmallNet vs. VGG16

When we made our basic decision tree classifier in the last chapter, we were able to use scikit-learn to get some statistics about model performance such as precision, recall, accuracy, AUC, and an ROC curve.

Since we need to get these statistics for both networks, we'll just create a single method that will automatically print these statistics and show relevant graphs:

INPUT[CELL=17]

```python
from sklearn.metrics import (roc_curve, auc,
classification_report,
RocCurveDisplay, confusion_matrix, ConfusionMatrixDisplay)

def get_stats(model, generator, model_name):
    preds = model.predict(generator)
    pred_classes = [1 if x >= 0.5 else 0 for x in preds]
    true_vals = generator.classes
    print("CLASSIFICATION REPORT")
    print(classification_report(true_vals, pred_classes,
    target_names=['normal','pn']))
    cm = confusion_matrix(true_vals, pred_classes)
    disp = ConfusionMatrixDisplay(confusion_matrix=cm,
    display_labels=['normal','pn'])
    disp.plot(values_format='')
    fpr, tpr, thresholds = roc_curve(true_vals, preds)
    auc_val = auc(fpr, tpr)
    print("AUC is ", auc_val)
    display = RocCurveDisplay(fpr, tpr, auc_val, model_name)
    display.plot()
    plt.show()
```

This method called `get_stats` takes in the trained model, a generator to run these statistics on (the test generator), and the name of the model which will be used in the plotting of the ROC curve.

The first line of the method gets the predictions of the model on the passed in generator (which will be our test generator). These predictions are values in the range of 0–1. For some of our statistics, we'll need to force these continuous decimal values to one class or another, so (in the second line), we use a list comprehension statement to loop through all of the prediction probabilities. If the prediction probability is >= 0.5, then we will say that it is class 1 (which is our pneumonia class); otherwise, it will be class 0. We store these prediction classes in the `pred_classes` variable. For our metrics, we also need the true classes of each of the values in our generator, which can be accessed using `generator.classes`.

Next, we're going to display a classification report. First, we print out to the user that there is a classification report coming. Next, we print out the results from the `classification_report` method in the scikit-learn metrics submodule. This method call takes in the true class labels, the predicted class labels, and what are the class names (a list).

We will also generate a confusion matrix using the `confusion_matrix` method (also from scikit-learn's metrics submodule). The confusion matrix method takes in the true class labels (stored in `true_values`) and our predicted classes (stored in `pred_classes`). However, if we want to actually see a confusion matrix plot (rather than the number of true positives, true negatives, false positives, and false negatives), we need to instantiate a `ConfusionMatrixDisplay` object (also comes from scikit-learn metrics), passing in the result of the confusion matrix call and a parameter `display_labels` with the names of our classes. We store the result of this ConfusionMatrixDisplay call in the variable `disp` and then call `disp.plot` passing in the argument `values_format=' '` to make sure that we print out the raw number (default is to print numbers in scientific notation).

Next, we'll want to print out the AUC and the ROC plot. To do so, we'll first call the `roc_curve` method from scikit, passing in the true class labels

(true_vals) and the prediction probabilities stored in preds (since the
ROC curve generation process needs access to the raw class probabilities).
The roc_curve method returns three values, a list of false positive rates,
a list of false negative rates, and a list with the associated probability
cutoff thresholds for each of those rates. We can get the AUC using the
auc method (passing in the fpr and tpr variables from the roc_curve
call) and then can print out the resulting AUC value. Lastly, we call the
RocCurveDisplay method to generate an ROC plot. This method only
requires the false positive rate and true positive rate lists, the AUC value,
and the name of the model (which will be displayed in a legend item next
to the AUC). We then call .plot() on the result from this call and show the
final plots.

Now that we've set up the method to print out evaluation metrics, let's
actually call the method. To give ourselves the best evaluation metrics,
let's use the model that had the lowest validation loss. In most cases, that
should be the current model variables you have (vgg_model and small_
model); however, in some cases, the most recent model state may not be
the best one. However, recall that we set up a ModelCheckpoint callback
that would only save a model on each epoch if it beat out the previous
epoch. That means that we have our best models saved to the Colab file
system and just need to load it into memory! Let's do that in the following
block of code:

INPUT[CELL=18]

```
small_model_ld = load_model('model_smallnet.hdf5')
vgg_model_ld = load_model('model_vgg.hdf5')
```

The load_model method is coming from the tensorflow.keras.models
submodule and takes in a file path to the model you want to load in. If
you look back at our ModelCheckpoint definition, it saves models under
the name model_{model_name}.hdf5, so we just need to pass in model_
smallnet.hdf5 to load in the best SmallNet model and pass in model_vgg.
hdf5 to load in the best VGG16 model.

We can get the model statistics as follows:

INPUT[CELL=19]

```
get_stats(vgg_model_ld, test_generator, "vgg")
```

OUTPUT

Refer to Figure 6-11 for the classification report from VGG16.

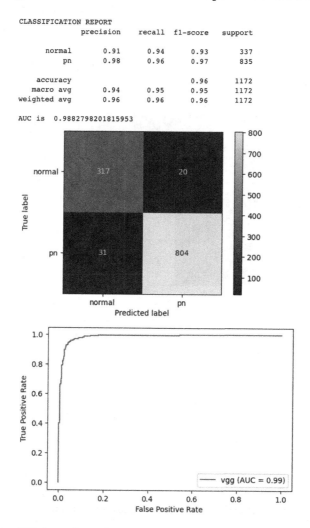

Figure 6-11. *VGG16 classification report*

INPUT[CELL=20]

```
get_stats(small_model, test_generator, "smallnet")
```

OUTPUT

Refer to Figure 6-12 for the classification report from SmallNet.

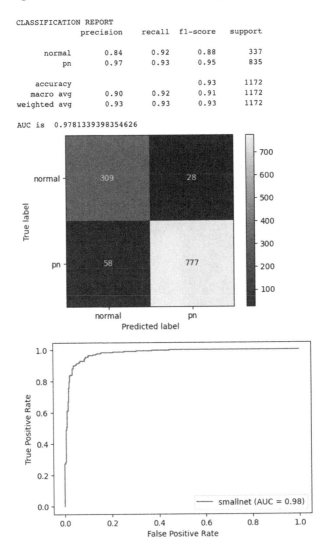

Figure 6-12. *SmallNet classification report*

As we can see from this report, the VGG net has a higher accuracy (0.96 vs. 0.93), precision for the "pn" (pneumonia) class (0.98 vs. 0.97), and recall (a.k.a. sensitivity) for the "pn" class (0.96 vs. 0.93). The AUC for the VGG network is 0.988 and is slightly higher than the AUC for the SmallNet network (0.978). In general, we would pick the VGG network for future usage since it exhibited better overall statistics in our use case. However, the Grad-CAM results from earlier would give some pause for determining whether it is actually generalizable (since VGG was focusing on the edges of images in addition to relevant anatomical locations).

At this point, it would probably be best to download both of your networks. They will be in the file tab of Colab and end with the file extension .hdf5 (which is what Keras uses to store the weights of the model). The smallnet model file is approximately 130 MB in size (which isn't too large); however, the VGG16 model is 1.3 GB in size which is huge! In general, as the size of the network increases, the file size containing the weights of that network will also increase (and accordingly, it'll take longer to load everything into computer memory/may push up against your computer's memory limits if it is very large).

Now that we've done a formal evaluation, let's see how we could use our model without defining generators.

Evaluating on "External" Images

Here is a self-enclosed code block that can give you the ability to output predictions for any image so long as the image is uploaded to the Colab file system:

INPUT[CELL=21]

```
from tensorflow.keras.preprocessing.image import load_img,
img_to_array
from tensorflow.keras.models import load_model
import numpy as np
```

```python
def predict_image(model, img_path):
  img = img_to_array(load_img(img_path,
  target_size=(224,224,3)))
  img = img * (1./255)
  img = np.expand_dims(img, axis=0)
  pred = model.predict(img)
  label = 'PNEUMONIA' if pred >= 0.5 else 'NORMAL'
  print("prediction: ", label, "P(Pneumonia): ", pred[0][0])
```

Some of these import statements are things we've already imported, but I'm just putting these here in case you want to skip to the end of the notebook and run a trained model. The first line of the method will load in an image and convert it to an array with the target size for our networks (in this case 224x224x3). We then need to multiply this image by 1/255 since we did this during the training process and our network has learned based on these rescaled images. Then, we'll expand the dimensions of the image to mimic the natural input of our network which is a batch. By calling np.expand_dims(img, axis=0), we're creating a fake batch with just one image in it. At this point, the image can be fed into the model. predict method. We get the prediction probability and store it in pred and then create an interpretable label (either pneumonia or normal based on whether the probability is >= 0.5 or not). Lastly, we print out these predictions to the screen.

To execute the method, we run the following code:

INPUT[CELL=22]

```python
m = load_model('model_smallnet.hdf5')
predict_image(m, 'chest_xray/train/NORMAL/IM-0410-0001.jpeg')
```

OUTPUT

```
prediction:  NORMAL P(Pneumonia):  0.0043188934
```

We needed to load in the model into memory first (so you would need to have it uploaded back to the Colab notebook if you got disconnected). Then we just call the predict_image method, passing in the loaded model and the path to image.

With that, we're done!

Things to Improve

Our model is by no means perfect (as we saw from our Grad-CAM results). Furthermore, some of the contestants in the Kaggle competition using the chest x-ray images pointed out that the test dataset has some mislabeled images, possibly biasing our overall accuracy statistics. Additionally, we also saw that our training and test sets had a class imbalance, in the direction of more pneumonia images. In the real clinical setting, it may be more likely that we have a plurality of normal x-ray images but not very many pneumonia images. We could have adjusted for this class imbalance by passing in a class_weights argument to the model.fit call in our fit_model method (you should check out the Keras documentation on how to do this!). The class weights method would give more weight to an underrepresented class so the network behaves as if both classes have similar distributions in the dataset.

To fix our Grad-CAM issues, we can try to continue training our network as follows:

```
vgg_model_cont, vgg_model_hist_cont = fit_model
(train_generator,
    validation_generator, 'vgg', epochs=100,
    model_fname='model_vgg.hdf5')
```

This will continue training the version of the model we have stored in model_vgg.hdf5 for another 100 epochs. We can continue even longer; however, Colab will randomly stop execution if you are using the Colab environment for a long period of time (the free tier only allows 12 hours of computation at a single time). Also, if our validation loss isn't decreasing, our EarlyStopping callback will kick in to stop training, making sure that we aren't overfitting.

There are some additional "wish list" items that would take a fair amount of time to implement, but are nonetheless necessary for usage in the medical sphere. First, our input images are .jpg files; however, most of the x-ray files are saved in a format called "DICOM" images. There are Python libraries out there such as pydicom that will allow you to read in raw DICOM files. However, the process of getting these images to something that can be used isn't so straightforward since DICOM images contain pixel values that have intensities in the 10,000+ value range, far about the 255 max for any regular image. We can use something like the following lines of code to convert DICOM images to PNGs which can then be used in our training pipeline:

```python
import pydicom
from PIL import Image
import numpy as np
import cv2

def read_dicom_to_png(image_path):
    ds = pydicom.dcmread()
    img = np.array(Image.fromarray(ds.pixel_array))
    mean, std = img.mean(), img.std()
    img = np.clip((img-mean)/std, -2.5, 2.5)
    img = ((img - img.min()) * (1/(img.max() - img.min()) *
    255)).astype(np.uint8)
    img = cv2.cvtColor(img, cv2.COLOR_GRAY2BGR)
    cv2.imwrite('output.png', img)
```

Going roughly line by line, we read in the image using `pydicom.dcmread()`. We then convert the resultant pixel values (stored in `ds.pixel_array`) into an image object and convert that into an array (using `np.array(Image.fromarray(...))`. We need to do this step since the image manipulation libraries in Python don't natively understand dicom pixel values. We then get the mean and standard decision of the image (with `img.mean()` and `img.std()`) and "clip" (i.e., set bounds) any pixel values 2.5 standard deviations above/below the mean (using `np.clip`). These values will then be mapped to the range 1–255 using the formula in the fifth line of our method. We will then convert the image to a three-channel color image using `cv2.cvtColor`. Lastly, we'll write the image to disk using `cv2.imwrite`.

There are other image formats to be aware of (such as NifTI images); however, they'll all follow the same general set of steps to convert images into something you can use to train your networks (i.e., load format-specific image using format reader library, convert to image array, clip values, rescale to 1–255, convert to color image, save).

Lastly, another "wish list" item would be to get a radiologist's opinion on the accuracy of the network predictions. Ideally, if we have a team of radiologists viewing these images as well, we can assess inter-rater reliability (via Kappa statistics) to determine if the radiologists agree with each other and whether those results agree with the network predictions or not.

Recap

We've made enormous strides in this chapter. In the process of setting all this up, we learned how to load in image data, clean it, and use generators to augment our image data. We then went through the process of constructing a convolutional neural network from scratch, implementing the concepts we covered in Chapter 4 in the process. Through constructing

SmallNet, we saw what convolution operations did to our image size and the overall number of parameters we learned. We also explored concepts such as loss functions and activation functions. We then demonstrated how we could use callbacks to monitor our training process and alter things like learning rate to encourage further training progress or even halt the training process altogether. We then went on to use transfer learning to repurpose VGG16 from detecting 1000 different image classes to our pneumonia classification task. We lastly trained these networks and evaluated their accuracy, precision, recall, and AUC in addition to seeing how they "think" (i.e., visualizing the outputs with Grad-CAM).

Now that we know exactly how these convolutional neural networks are created and what they can actually do, let's discuss other areas of ML for you to learn on your own, general considerations to keep in mind while implementing AI algorithms in the medical field, and how to continue learning on your own.

CHAPTER 7

The Future of Healthcare and AI

Over the past couple of chapters, we've gone through the code of what makes something "AI," but all of this content is just a small sample of the world of ML/AI in general. Though a lot of the tools you use to make these algorithms will be the same (such as scikit-learn, Keras, and TensorFlow), the implementations will be vastly different depending on the task. However, the general structure we set up for making deep learning models (i.e., make generators ➤ define model ➤ define callbacks ➤ train) does apply to a number of different deep learning-based tasks. Since we don't have time to talk about everything in this chapter, we'll instead talk about how to start your own projects, how to understand errors, and what to do when you encounter those errors.

Stepping outside of the realm of concepts directly related to coding, we'll wrap up our chapter with three sections related to concepts you should consider when developing and deploying these algorithms to the real world. Concepts such as how to protect patient privacy are incredibly relevant these days, especially as medical imaging tasks require lots of data to run correctly. Accordingly, we need to ensure that people's information is protected in the process/they agree that their information can be used in the training of algorithms. We'll then move on to covering some caveats associated with ML in the medical sphere, including general guidelines on how to spot "AI snake oil" and preventing algorithmic bias (a concept that

© Abhinav Suri 2022
A. Suri, *Practical AI for Healthcare Professionals*,
https://doi.org/10.1007/978-1-4842-7780-5_7

describes how programs can prove to be detrimental to some individuals). Lastly, we'll cover some of the things that you should report if you choose to take on AI research and deploy trained models to the real world.

Starting Your Own Projects

Most of the content in this book isn't only available in the book itself. Everything I've laid out here comes from a combination of code documentation, question and answer forums online, tutorials/guides written by companies doing AI work, and some of my prior classes. Needless to say, it is very hard (and arguably pointless) to actually create truly "original" code. Most of the things that you are aiming to do will exist online in some form or another; however, it is up to you to find what tools exist online and how those tools can be adapted to the problem you're trying to solve.

Take the chest x-ray classification problem. If you look up online how to detect pneumonia in chest x-ray images using AI, you'll likely be directed to some research papers and the Kaggle competition where the dataset lives. You could take a look through some of the competition code (will be available under the "Code" tab for most Kaggle competitions); however, you may find yourself wading through a lot of poorly documented code that is fairly opaque and difficult to read.

Instead, you could try and generalize your problem. There's arguably nothing special about the fact that our input images are chest x-rays, and we want to find out if it is pneumonia or not. Rather, we could generalize and say "I want some ML/AI algorithm that can take in an image and output a classification." If you type in "ML/AI image classification tutorial keras" into Google, you'll get a lot of well-documented code examples and tutorials running you through exactly how to make a classifier neural network. If you add "transfer learning" to that search query, you'll likely find mentions about VGG16 as well. It is up to you to actually determine how to a) choose the tutorial (or tutorials) that you'd like to follow and b) adapt the tutorial code to fit your purpose. Regardless, the key lesson is that generalizing your problem can lead you to find something that can be adapted to your use case.

Debugging

Okay, now let's say that you've found a tutorial that shows you how to use VGG16 to classify images and you start writing up the code. However, when you start running things, you start seeing messages being printed out containing the word "error." Let's take a look at an example of what that error might look like:

INPOUT

```
def make_network(network_name):
    print("making model", networkname)

make_network('vgg')
```

OUTPUT

```
-----------------------------------------------------------------
NameError                                    Traceback (most
                                             recent call last)
<ipython-input-1-699ebc7cd358> in <module>()
      2     print("making model", networkname)
      3
----> 4 make_network('vgg')

<ipython-input-1-699ebc7cd358> in make_network(network_name)
      1 def make_network(network_name):
----> 2     print("making model", networkname)
      3
      4 make_network('vgg')

NameError: name 'networkname' is not defined
```

This message seems rather cryptic and confusing. However, let's take a look and see what this error message is telling us. In general, the best way to read an error from Python is to start at the bottom. In this case "NameError: name 'networkname' is not defined." Okay, so Python seems to think that the variable "networkname" doesn't exist (i.e., it is not defined). Alright, but don't we define it by passing in a value into the make_ network method? Okay, let's look at the next line above the "NameError" line. Hmm, so it seems like there is a networkname being mentioned in our print statement, but wait, it seems like networkname is not the same as network_name. It seems that we have made a typo! If we went further up the error message, we would see exactly what method calls resulted in the error happening (in this case, the call to make_network('vgg')). But since we know that there's an error due to a typo, we can just find our method to be the following:

```
def make_network(network_name):
    print("making model", network_name)

make_network('vgg')
```

And everything will work as intended.

There are also cases when it becomes very difficult if not impossible to actually interpret the error message yourself. At that point, it would be best for you to turn to Google and, in particular, a website called StackOverflow. However, it does take a little bit of experimentation to get to the point that you can type your error into Google and get back something sensical. Here are some general guidelines on how to format your questions:

1. Remove all specific information. If we typed in "NameError: name 'networkname' is not defined" into Google, we're probably going to get a lot of "false positive" results from stack overflow dealing with Internet networks rather than neural networks. That's because we made our query too specific. The

likelihood that some other programmer came up with the exact same variable naming scheme and had the exact same NameError pop up is incredibly low. Instead, if you type in "NameError: name is not defined," you might get some more results since all NameError messages will have those words in common.

2. If you think that a library that you are using is involved, type that into your query as well. In this case, we aren't using any special libraries or calling any methods on our libraries, so it wouldn't make any sense for us to add things. But if we came across any other error after running a scikit-learn function, it would be best to format your query as "General Error Message Here, scikit learn."

3. In the case that you aren't able to find anything earlier, you could potentially open up a new question on stack overflow and hope that someone takes notice to answer it. To do so, you should open up a stack overflow account and ask a question. In the question body, you should provide as much information you can about the script you are running, what you did to invoke that script/method, and any additional data you are using to help others reproduce the problem. You should also paste in the exact error message that pops up. Most of the individuals on these forums want to help others, but they need question askers to do their fair share of the work and give enough information so no one is wasting their time going back and forth to get more information.

In the worst case scenario, you may find yourself without any help in figuring out what's going wrong. Though this situation is rare (it's more indicative of the fact that it may be difficult to word your question in a manner that would return search results), it is still something you should know how to handle. When I find myself in this situation, I have always found that recoding the method or segment of code, using different variable names, and only going one segment at a time are incredibly beneficial. It forces you to take a step back and examine everything line by line.

There are also some more insidious errors that can arise, such as those when training or evaluating ML algorithms. For example, when I wrote the code to evaluate SmallNet and VGG16, I kept on getting accuracies and AUCs that were very far off from the validation AUC/accuracy of the last epoch of the network (validation AUC 0.97 vs. final AUC of 0.54). My stack overflow queries included the following:

- "AUC calculation sklearn vs. Keras"

- "Keras validation AUC different from sklearn AUC"

- "Test Generator AUC Keras far off from validation"

It was that last query that clued me into the real solution to the problem. But my first two queries were motivated by the initial thought that the AUC that Keras calculates in the callback metrics was using a different algorithm than the AUC calculated by scikit-learn called in our evaluation method. While those searches did yield some information that indicated that Keras and scikit implement AUC calculations differently, I didn't see something that explains the very large difference in AUCs I was noticing. I then saw that the evaluation code I was using was using the test generator and decided to look into whether a generator shuffles data. That could contribute to how our AUC dropped to 0.54 (which is the equivalent of randomly guessing). The running hypothesis was that when I passed in the test generator and called the model.predict method, the test generator may have shuffled values, and then, when I got the actual class names, I would have been getting the newly shuffled class names rather than the original ones associated with the images I wanted to predict. Sure enough, I came across a stack overflow answer that said "Make sure you set shuffle=False on your generator." It turns out that generators have a `shuffle=True` parameter enabled by default, and I forgot to set `shuffle=False` on the test set in the code. Once I did that, the evaluation results matched with the validation results!

That was an example of a logical error. It is an error that may not yield any actual program errors, but produces unexpected results. The best way to deal with those errors is to start out with the most likely hypotheses and start to go down into more and more specific ones. Again, re-implementing your code may help here, but also going through the documentation for all the methods you call can be very useful.

Speaking of going through the documentation, here's an example of what you could expect to see (refer to Figure 7-1).

`flow_from_dataframe` **method**

```
ImageDataGenerator.flow_from_dataframe(
    dataframe,
    directory=None,
    x_col="filename",
    y_col="class",
    weight_col=None,
    target_size=(256, 256),
    color_mode="rgb",
    classes=None,
    class_mode="categorical",
    batch_size=32,
    shuffle=True,
    seed=None,
    save_to_dir=None,
    save_prefix="",
    save_format="png",
    subset=None,
    interpolation="nearest",
    validate_filenames=True,
    **kwargs
)
```

Takes the dataframe and the path to a directory + generates batches.

The generated batches contain augmented/normalized data.

A simple tutorial can be found here.

Arguments

- **dataframe**: Pandas dataframe containing the filepaths relative to `directory` (or absolute paths if `directory` is None) of the images in a string column. It should include other column/s depending on the `class_mode`: - if `class_mode` is "categorical" (default value) it must include the `y_col` column with the class/es of each image. Values in column can be string/list/tuple if a single class or list/tuple if multiple classes. - if `class_mode` is "binary" or "sparse" it must include the given `y_col` column with class values as strings. - if `class_mode` is "raw" or "multi_output" it should contain the columns specified in `y_col`. - if `class_mode` is "input" or None no extra column is needed.
- **directory**: string, path to the directory to read images from. If None, data in `x_col` column should be absolute paths.

Figure 7-1. *Documentation from* https://keras.io/api/
preprocessing/image/#flowfromdataframe-method

Here, you can see an example of how to call this method and the list of default arguments (any arguments that have a keyword=value pair listed). If you don't manually specify a new value for those default arguments, the program will assume you want to use the defaults. Following the code, there will be a short description of the method followed by the list of arguments with associated descriptions. If you're lucky, you may find that some library authors go so far as to give you example code that uses the method itself.

In the case that documentation for a library is minimal, chances are that some other people might have used the library before. You can leverage the power of GitHub, a website that hosts open source code, to search through people's prior usage of that code. Just type in a method name into the search bar, and click the "Code" tab of results. Any publicly available code that contains that phrase will show up in the code results, and you can see how they actually use it. In this case, we see that querying for flow_from_dataframe on GitHub turns up as a result that has code associated with a repository (a.k.a. a project) titled Medical_Image_Analysis which could lead us to look at their code a bit more for inspiration. Refer to Figure 7-2 for some example search results you could expect to see.

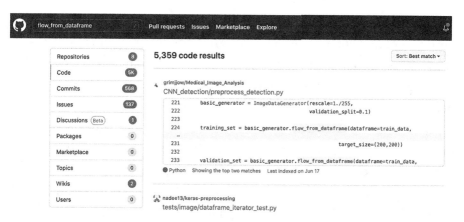

Figure 7-2. *Example code search results from GitHub*

You can also attempt to copy code if you are really stuck, but only do so if you truly understand what is going on. Also, if you are going to take some code from GitHub, visit the repository first and check out a file called

237

"LICENSE.txt." That will outline exactly what you can do with that code and what rights you have to reproduce it (if any).

Now that we've spent some time in the weeds figuring out how to make projects on our own and learning how to debug, let's start to consider the implications of AI and subjects that must be considered while making AI-based solutions in medicine.

Considerations

This is by no means a comprehensive list of considerations one should take whenever determining whether or not to pursue an AI-based project; however, it touches on some of the most pressing topics in the AI sphere right now.

Patient Privacy

When we talk about patient privacy in the medical context, the number one concept that comes to mind is HIPAA. Though it may not apply to all use cases, the guidelines that HIPAA advocates for in terms of security and data anonymization still should apply to any projects taking on the medical applications of AI. Above all, patient privacy protections should be put into place to not only ensure that AI developers do not leak data to the outside world but also to ensure that the algorithm does not learn on private patient data that would render it useless in the real world.

What exact protections should be put in place to ensure patient privacy? First, any identifying imaging information should be stripped from imaging headers. For example, by default, DICOM files will record information about the patient identification number, the patient's age, date of birth, and weight unless configured otherwise. Data used to train neural networks will often reside on someone's computer or server; non-anonymized DICOM headers could prove to be very useful to any malicious actors who want to access data. In addition to scrubbing information from DICOM headers and other relevant clinical files, the servers and hard disks that this data resides on should be encrypted and password protected with a tightly controlled access list.

In terms of training an algorithm, it is entirely possible that the algorithm itself can actually "leak" information to the outside world just through regular use. Some machine learning algorithms, such as natural language processing algorithms (NLP), generate "new" data as its output. For example, NLP algorithms can be used to do text generation (e.g., generate medical notes); however, NLP algorithms that are overfit to their training data could just be leaking some bits of that training data which can be used to identify individuals. Carefully choosing what algorithms to train and making sure that information is not being overfit can prove to be useful in combatting this issue.

Speaking of areas where the ML algorithm produces counterintuitive results, let's talk about algorithmic bias.

Algorithmic Bias

Algorithmic bias refers to the idea that AI algorithms (and other procedural algorithms) can produce biased results. Particularly in the context of race and social inequality, algorithmic bias is a major concern while training medically relevant machine learning algorithms today. To see why this may be an issue, consider the situation where we may be training a classifier to detect melanomas on the skin.

To train our network, we may turn to popular online imaging repositories of moles. We download this repository of images, create a classifier just as we did for the pneumonia dataset, and then evaluate its accuracy. It turns out to be over 90% accurate which is great. We then take this trained algorithm to our hospital system/dermatologists and ask them to use it, and they end up reporting that the algorithm produces predictions on melanoma status that agree with the dermatologist, but only for individuals with lighter skin. When the patient had darker skin, the algorithm completely failed to produce valid results. We might try to find reasons why this may be. Perhaps the lighting was bad, but that seems to be unlikely. Then we turn to the original dataset and find that the vast majority of images were from light-skinned individuals. We have, perhaps unintentionally, made a biased algorithm. The bias arose from the fact that the training data was not representative of the true patient population and our network, accordingly, learned that bias in its training process.

To help combat bias, we should try to stratify the evaluation of our algorithms across a variety of demographics in our ultimate patient population. In this situation, we can use the Fitzpatrick skin type scale to assign each patient a skin tone (I = lightest, VI = darkest) and evaluate the accuracy of classification for each category. From there, we can use a Cochran-Armitage trend test (or any other statistical test of your choice) to determine if there is a significant trend (e.g., accuracy goes down as category number increases) or not.

This situation isn't just theoretical; this is an issue that is playing out in the real world right now. Google rolled out an application called "Derm Assist" in March of 2021. The results of it have yet to be seen; however, researchers are already raising concerns about its ability to work in individuals who have darker skin tones since the images used to train the dataset only have (as far as we know) 2.7% type V skin tones and < 1% type VI skin tones. While we don't know the ultimate efficacy of this predictive application, we can think of some ways to prevent algorithmic bias from affecting end users.

The first way is to prevent bias in our datasets from happening in the first place. To do this, we need to be mindful about what policies may cause someone to contribute to the dataset vs. not contribute. For example, if data used to train the algorithm is volunteered, we should make sure that volunteers are all able to contribute data without barriers in their way (e.g., lack of technology, lack of time, etc.). We could also make sure to get our data from several different hospital systems rather than a single hospital since some hospitals may be located in areas that are not socioeconomically or racially diverse.

The second way to prevent bias is to selectively augment underrepresented cases in our dataset. While the programmatic way to do this is beyond the scope of this chapter, there are several image augmentation libraries out there (such as `imgaug`) that will allow you to specify how often some image should be augmented based on its characteristics. If we find that a particular group is underrepresented in our dataset, we could use this method to increase its representation in the dataset overall.

The last way to prevent bias is to make sure that evaluation is done on an entirely separate holdout set rather than a testing set that was part of the same data you used originally. Though doing this is more time consuming (as you'll need to find multiple datasets), it should validate the performance of your algorithm on a set of patients it was never actually trained on, potentially exposing shortcomings in your algorithm in general. If you do not have access to another dataset, you could create a limited rollout of your algorithm and monitor results across demographic subgroups to determine how it is operating before launching it to the general public.

Now that we've covered algorithmic bias and how it could produce unexpected results, let's talk about how AI-based solutions can overpromise yet under-deliver in the real world.

Snake Oil + Creating Trust in the Real World

One of the upsides and downsides of AI is the fact that there is a lot of funding associated with solutions that employ AI, especially in the medical field. However, nefarious actors have started to claim that their technology uses "AI" when it really doesn't, or they even go so far as to tout an AI solution to a problem that has a well-known algorithmic solution already. Unfortunately, some hospital administrators have fallen prey to these claims and end up wasting millions of dollars.

In general, these snake-oil claims operate on the "hype" associated with AI in the past few years. News cycles that are taken up by algorithms that can do things like reverse image searching and facial recognition can easily lead the public to think that AI is already tackling "hard" problems and can be easily extended to do medical diagnosis at the level of a physician. While AI systems are actually exceeding the accuracy of some physicians, they only tend to do so in very specific subtasks (such as pneumonia detection on x-ray images).

But how do we actually predict snake oil claims? We can go back to the earlier parts of this section: generalizing the problem. Let's take a popular AI problem that is believed to be bordering on snake oil (with a slight medical twist): predicting physician job success prior to a physician being hired. What would the inputs and outputs be to our training algorithm? The inputs would probably be various characteristics of current providers at the time they were hired and the outputs would be their job success (perhaps measured in terms of % salary increase after a set period of time). It is possible that an algorithm could have been trained to predict this with high accuracy, but where would the data be coming from? It would likely be coming from a few healthcare systems, or, perhaps more likely, the developer company itself. At that point, we need to ask questions about the validity of the algorithm in our use case (as covered in the algorithmic bias section). Furthermore, we need to realize the network will only predict "accurate" outcomes for individuals who were actually hired by company/ healthcare system, and thus, it may not perform well at other healthcare systems/companies that have different valued skills among providers.

In order to generate trust in the real world, it is necessary to try and explain as much about the AI process as possible. Concepts such as the general ML algorithm used for the task, the data used to train the algorithm, and its evaluation statistics are all essential to report. Wherever possible, model outputs should be explained to some extent (just as we showed in our Grad-CAM results from the previous chapter). The last point is especially valued in the medical world since AI still tends to be treated as "black box" that has no degree explainability.

Speaking of explaining, let's talk about how to talk about AI in general when you're in the situation of leading an AI-based project in your healthcare system.

How to Talk About AI

In some cases, you may find yourself in the position where you are either directly implementing an AI algorithm or are in charge of doing telling others what the aims of the project are. When working with programmers, it is important to be as explicit as possible. Let's walk through an example of how to specify a problem: our chest x-ray classification problem from the last chapter. If we're explaining what we want to do to a programmer, these are the questions we'll need to have answers to:

- What is the goal of this project?

  To predict pneumonia status from chest x-ray images.

- What is the input and output for this AI? Do you have any suggestions for a potential architecture?

  The input will be chest x-ray images and the output should be a single world "NORMAL" or "PNEUMONIA" with a confidence level (ranging from 0 to 1) attached to it. It would also be nice to show exactly what parts of the image contributed the most to the ultimate classification decision. Since this is an image classification problem, it is probably best to use a convolutional neural network or something similar that is good at classifying images.

- What data will be used to train this network? How can
  I download it? What is its general format? Is this data
  already labeled? Can I trust the labels?

  We will be using the Kaggle chest x-ray dataset. These
  can be downloaded from the Kaggle competition
  website (send them a link). The images are .jpg files
  and do not need any additional processing before they
  can be used as inputs to a neural network (if they were
  DICOM images, you should specify that here). They are
  already labeled as normal vs. pneumonia, and images
  are already in folders labeled with the appropriate
  class. The labels can be trusted in most cases, but it is
  likely that we need to get another physician to look at
  the test data and make sure that it is accurate.

- What metric do we want to optimize?

  We want to optimize accuracy, but also want to make
  sure that we have very minimal false negatives (i.e.,
  we want a very high sensitivity) since it would be
  deleterious to miss a pneumonia case.

- Where will this network actually be run? Who is the
  person I can contact to get it to run in that setting?
  What are the constraints of that platform?

  Ideally, we would like to have this network integrated
  into our PACS system so it can give us predictions
  instantly without us needing to execute a separate
  script. Person X can tell you what you need to do to get
  your outputs into a format that can be understandable.
  (Note this wasn't covered in the last chapter; however,
  this is also a major pain point for developers since not
  everyone is going to be running Colab notebooks to

get outputs from your network. In some cases, PACS systems may not allow separate scripts to be executed, which makes the programmer's job difficult. In this situation, it may be best to compromise by saying that you'd be willing to train physicians how to use any custom piece of software the developer makes.)

- Will you need this network to continue to be trained? How will you identify which new training samples to add?

  Yes, we would like this network to continue to be trained. Ideally, any application with this model should flag results where the model does not agree with the physician and use that case as a training sample. (Note, we didn't cover this explicitly in the last chapter, but you can continue to train a network on a different dataset as well; you just need a new train generator made).

Once you answer these questions, you should be able to get to the point that you can specify exactly what you need from a developer who is working on your project. Much of the development pain points that come up in the programming process usually are due to misunderstood expectations, and being explicitly clear about these solutions can lead you to the point that you can provide your developer with enough information to do their task.

Wrap Up

As we've seen in this chapter and the prior chapters, AI is not really magic, and we can understand how these programs learn and produce the results that they do. While this book didn't touch much on the potential of AI in general, the concepts covered in programming/computer science topics, some basic ML algorithm types, and implementation details for ML and deep learning algorithms will provide enough of a basis for you to start exploring on your own. Even with the two major projects covered in this book, a whole world of medical research is open to you. With scikit-learn and PyCaret, you can evaluate a different dataset and try and optimize a classification task. With TensorFlow and Keras, you can use transfer learning to run image classification on a disease that has not been covered in medical imaging literature yet. With the skills established in the last chapter, you'll also be ahead of your peers and know what to look out for when evaluating AI solutions that are presented to you. You even have some basic examples of what answers to have prepared when taking on an AI-based project yourself.

Overall, this book is meant to serve as a seed for further knowledge growth, and I hope that you can continue learning how to use some of the AI-based algorithms out there to benefit patients in the medical setting.

Index

Printed in the United States
by Baker & Taylor Publisher Services